GENDER DYNAMICS IN INDIA

AF795227

Sandhya Rani Das

First Edition: 2010

Himalaya Publishing House

MUMBAI • NEW DELHI • NAGPUR • BENGALURU • HYDERABAD • CHENNAI • PUNE • LUCKNOW • AHMEDABAD • ERNAKULAM • BHUBANESWAR • INDORE • KOLKATA

© Author

No part of this publication may be reproduced, stored in a retrieval system, or transmitted in any form or by any means, electronic, mechanical, photocopying, recording and/or otherwise without the prior written permission of the author and the publisher.

First Edition : 2010

Published by : Mrs. Meena Pandey for **Himalaya Publishing House Pvt. Ltd.,** "Ramdoot", Dr. Bhalerao Marg, Girgaon, **Mumbai - 400 004.** Phone: .022-2386 01 70/2386 38 63, Fax: 022-2387 71 78 **Email: himpub@vsnl.com Website: www.himpub.com**

Branch Offices:

New Delhi : "Pooja Apartments", 4-B, Murari Lal Street, Ansari Road, Darya Ganj, New Delhi - 110 002. Phone: 011-23270392/23278631, Fax: 011-23256286

Nagpur : Kundanlal Chandak Industrial Estate, Ghat Road, Nagpur - 440 018. Phone: 0712-2738731/3296733, Telefax: 0712-2721215

Bengaluru : No. 16/1 (Old 12/1), 1st Floor, Next to Hotel Highlands, Madhava Nagar, Race Course Road, Bengaluru - 560 001. Phone: 080-22281541/22385461, Telefax: 080-22286611

Hyderabad : No. 3-4-184, Lingampally, Besides Raghavendra Swamy Matham, Kachiguda, Hyderabad - 500 027. Phone: 040-27560041/27550139, Mobile: 09848130433

Chennai : No. 85/50, Bazullah Road, T. Nagar, Chennai - 600 017. Phone: 044-28344020/32463737/42124860

Pune : First Floor, "Laksha" Apartment, No. 527, Mehunpura, Shaniwarpeth (Near Prabhat Theatre), Pune - 411 030. Phone: 020-24496323/24496333

Lucknow : Jai Baba Bhavan, Church Road, Near Manas Complex and Dr. Awasthi Clinic, Aliganj, Lucknow - 226 024. Phone: 0522-2339329, Mobile:- 09305302158/09415349385/09389593752

Ahmedabad : 114, "SHAIL", 1st Floor, Opp. Madhu Sudan House, C.G.Road, Navrang Pura, Ahmedabad - 380 009. Phone: 079-26560126, Mobile: 09327324149/09314679413

Ernakulam : 39/104 A, Lakshmi Apartment, Karikkamuri Cross Rd., Ernakulam, Cochin – 622011, Kerala. Phone: 0484-2378012/2378016, Mobile: 09344199799

Bhubaneswar : 5 Station Square, Bhubaneswar (Orissa) - 751 001. Mobile: 09861046007, E-mail: orissa@himpub.com

Indore : Kesardeep Avenue Extension, 73, Narayan Bagh, Flat No. 302, IIIrd Floor, Near Humpty Dumpty School, Narayan Bagh, Indore-452 007(M.P.), Mobile: 09301386468

Kolkata : 108/4, Beliaghata Main Road, Near ID Hospital, Opp. SBI Bank, Kolkata - 700 010, Mobile: 09910440956

DTP by : HPH Editorial Office, Bhandup (Priyanka)

Printed by : Shri Krishna offset Press Delhi-

PREFACE

For centuries women in India have been suffering due to discrimination, exploitation and exposure to various kinds of harassment at various levels. Women constitute nearly half of the total population of the country and the development of the country is not possible without the development of this vast segment. Today, the development of women has been a major concern for our planners and policy makers. After independence, our planners have envisaged various constitutional provisions to protect the interest of women and undertaken various socio-economic development measures for their upliftment. In addition, various voluntary organizations have also been working hard for emancipation of women. Despite all these efforts by the government and voluntary bodies, majority of women are deprived of their minimum rights.

By the middle of twentieth century and in the beginning of twenty first century, the women folk have been conscious about their rights and are gradually coming out of traditional bridle. Growth of education have given them the power to fight for their rights in the society. In this context, empowerment of women as a goal of women's development has been gaining wider acceptance. The book is an effort in compiling the hazards and achievements of women in general and Indian women in particular. The book deals in detail the health and education which is regarded as the most important indicator for the empowerment of women. The book also analyses the employment of women and present revolution of micro-finance which is a driving force for economic empowerment of women. The book also focuses on political participation of women which is necessary to regulate specific state policies towards empowerment of women. Nationally and internationally around the world with economic development, violence is fast growing and more and more women are facing a hazardous life which is truly reflected in the book.

The book is designed for the students of Women Studies, Economics and those scholars who are pursuing their research in gender studies. I hope that this book will meet the need of a text/reference book for the students as well as scholars.

Author

ACKNOWLEDGEMENTS

At the outset, I would like to thank the team of Himalaya Publishing House for giving me an opportunity to write this book. I also express my deep sense of gratitude to Prof. R. P. Sarma, Director, Institute of Economic Studies, Berhampur for going through the entire manuscript and giving many valuable suggestions. I am also thankful to the entire staff of Delhi School of Professional Studies and Research namely, Mr. R. S. Rajpoot, Mr. Mathura Prasad, Miss Neelam, and Miss Gayatri, for providing immense support for the completion of the book. Last but not least I thank my husband for his encouragement and moral support.

I would also like to express my special gratitude to the large number of authors whose work I have incorporated in my book. Any suggestion, feedback or recommendation is heartily welcome.

Author

CONTENTS

Chapter 1

INDIAN WOMEN

In ancient India, the women enjoyed equal status with men in all fields of life. Works by ancient Indian grammarians such as Patanjali and Katyayana suggest that women were educated in the early Vedic period. Rig Vedic verses suggest that the women married at a mature age and were free to select their husbands. Scriptures such as Rig Veda and Upanishads mention several women sages and seers, notably Gargi and Maitreyi. Women enjoyed equal status and rights during the early Vedic period. However, later(approximately 500 B.C.), the status of women began to decline with the Smritis (esp., Manusmriti) and other religious texts curtailing women's freedom and rights.

The Indian woman's position in the society further deteriorated during the medieval period. Sati, child marriages and ban on widow remarriages became part of social life in India. The Muslim conquest in the Indian subcontinent brought the *purdah* practice in the Indian society. Among the Rajputs of Rajasthan, the Jauhar was practised. In some parts of India, the Devadasis or the temple women were sexually exploited. Polygamy was widely practised especially among Hindu Kshatriya rulers.

In spite of these conditions, some women were excelled in the fields of politics, literature, education and religion. Razia Sultana became the only woman monarch to have ever ruled Delhi. The Gond Queen Durgavati ruled for fifteen years, before she lost her life in a battle with Mughal emperor Akbar's general Asaf Khan in 1564. Chand Bibi defended Ahmednagar against the mighty Mughal forces of Akbar in 1590s. Jehangir's wife Nur Jehan effectively wielded imperial power and was recognized as the real force behind the Mughal throne. Shivaji's wife, Jijibai was deputed as queen regent, because of her ability as a warrior and administrator. In South India, many women administered villages, towns, divisions and heralded social and religious institutions.

The Bhakti cults tried to restore women's status and questioned some of the forms of oppression. Mirabai, a female saint-poet,was one of the most important

Bhakti movement figures. Some other female saint-poets from this period include Akkamadevi, Rami Janabai and Lal Ded. Shortly after the Bhakti movement, Guru Nanak, the first guru of Sikhs also preached the message of equality between men and women. He advocated that women are allowed to lead religious assemblies; to perform and lead congregational hymn singing called Kirtan or Bhajan; become members of religious management committees; to lead armies on the battlefield; have equality in marriage,and equality in Amrit (Baptism). Other Sikh Gurus also preached the discrimination of women.

Historical Practices

Traditions such as (1) *Sati*, (2) Jauhar, (3) Child marriage, and (4) devadasi system have been banned and are largely defunct. However, some cases of these practices are still found in remote parts of India. The *purdah* is still practised by many middle-class Indian women in rural areas.

Sati System

Sati is an old, largely defunct custom, in which the widow was immolated alive on her husband's funeral pyre. Although the act was supposed to be a voluntary on the widow's part, it is believed to have been sometimes forced on the widow. It was abolished by the British in 1829. There have been forty reported cases of *sati* since independence. In 1987, the Roop Kanwar case of Rajasthan led to the Commission of Sati (Prevention) Act.

Practice of Jauhar

Jauhar refers to the practice of the voluntary immolation of all the wives and daughters of defeated warriors, in order to avoid capture and consequent molestation by the enemy. The practice was followed by the wives of defeated Rajput rulers, who are known to place a high premium on honour. Even in the modern world this system is still fooled in some part of India on religious ground.

Child Marriages

Earlier, child marriages were highly prevalent in India. The young girls would live with their parents till they reached puberty. In the past, the child widows were condemned to a life of great agony, shaving heads, living in isolation, and shunned by the society. Although child marriage was outlawed in 1860, it is still a common practice in some underdeveloped areas of the country.

Purdah

Purdah is the practice of requiring women to cover their bodies so as to cover their skin and conceal their form. It does not, contrary to common beliefs, impose restrictions on mobility of women, curtailment of their right to interact freely and it is not a symbol of subordination of women. *Purdah* system is no more prevailing among the Hindu; it is now a declining tradition in India, but in some parts of the country it is practised mostly by Muslim ladies.

System of Devadasi

Devadasi is a religious practice in some parts of southern India, in which women are "married" to a deity or temple. The ritual was well established by the 10th Century A. D. In the later period, the illegitimate sexual exploitation of the devadasis became a norm in some parts of India. Even today some communities offer their daughters to the village deity as devadasi.

British Rule

European scholars observed in the 19th Century that Hindu women are "naturally chaste" and "more virtuous" than other women. During the British Raj, many reformers such as Ram Mohan Roy, Ishwar Chandra Vidyasagar, Jyotirao Phule, etc., fought for the upliftment of women. Raja Rammohan Roy's efforts led to the abolition of the *Sati* practice in 1829. Ishwar Chandra Vidyasagar's crusade for the improvement in condition of widows led to the Widow Remarriage Act of 1856. Many women reformers such as Pandita Ramabai also helped the cause of women upliftment. Rani Lakshmi Bai, the Queen of Jhansi, led the Indian Rebellion of 1857 against the British. She is now widely considered as a nationalist hero. Begum Hazrat Mahal, the co-ruler of Awadh, was another ruler who led the revolt of 1857. She refused the deals with the British and later retreated to Nepal. The Begums of Bhopal were also few of the notable female rulers during this period. They did not observe *purdah* and were trained in martial arts.

In 1917, the first women's delegation met the Secretary of State to demand women's political rights, supported by the Indian National Congress. The All-India Women's Education Conference was held in Pune in 1927. In 1929, the Child Marriage Restraint Act was passed, stipulating fourteen as the minimum age for a girl through the efforts of Mohhamed Ali Jinnah. Though Mahatma Gandhi himself married at the age of thirteen, he later urged people to boycott child marriages and called upon the young men to marry the child widows.

Women played an important role in India's independence struggle. Some of the famous freedom fighters include Bhikaji Cama, Dr. Annie Besant, Pritilata Waddedar, Vijayalakshmi Pandit, Rajkumari Amrit Kaur, Anjali Ammal, Aruna Asaf Ali, Sucheta Kriplani and Kasturba Gandhi. Other notable names include Muthulakshmi Reddy, Durgabai Deshmukh, etc. The Rani of Jhansi Regiment of Subhash Chandra Bose's Indian National Army consisted entirely of women including Captain Lakshmi Sehgal. Sarojini Naidu, a poet and a freedom fighter, was the first Indian woman to become the President of the Indian National Congress and the first woman to become the governor of a state in India.

Independent India

Women in India now participate in all activities such as education, politics, media, art and culture, service sectors, science and technology, etc. The Constitution of India guarantees Indian women some special provisions.

Article 14: equal rights with men,

Article 15(1), no discrimination by the state,

Article 16, equality of opportunity,

Article 39(d), equal pay for equal work

In addition, it allows special provisions to be made by the state

Article 15(3), in favour of women and children

Article 51(A)(e), renounces practices derogatory to the dignity of women

Article 42, for securing just and humane conditions of work and for maternity relief.

Women in 20th Century

The steady change in the status of women can be visualized by looking at the achievements of women during last one century in India.

1. 1905: Suzanne RD Tata the first Indian woman to drive a car.
2. 1916: The first women's university, SNDT Women's University, was founded on June 2, 1916 by the social reformer Dhondo Keshav Karve with just five students.
3. 1951: Prem Mathur becomes the first Indian woman commercial pilot of the Deccan Airways.
4. 1959: Anna Chandy becomes the first Indian woman Judge of High Court.
5. 1966: Captain Durga Banerjee becomes the first Indian woman pilot of the state airline, Indian Airlines.
6. 1966: Kamaladevi Chattopadhyay wins Ramon Magsaysay award for community leadership.
7. 1966: Indira Gandhi becomes the first woman Prime Minister of India.
8. 1970: Kamaljit Sandhu becomes the first Indian woman to win a Gold in the Asian Games.
9. 1972: Kiran Bedi becomes the first female recruit to join the Indian Police Service.
10. 1989: Justice M. Fathima Beevi becomes the first woman judge of the Supreme Court of India.
11. 1992: Priya Jhingan becomes the first lady cadet to join the Indian Army (later commissioned on March 6, 1993).
12. 1994: Harita Kaur Deol became the first Indian woman to perform a solo flight.

13. 1997: Kalpana Chawla becomes the first Indian woman to go into Space.
14. 2004: Punita Arora becomes the first woman in the Indian Army to do the highest rank of Lt. General.
15. 2005: Manndhir Rajput, a 34-year-old woman from Ludhiana, Punjab becomes the first Indian woman to become an engine driver of trains with the New South Wales Rail Corporation, Australia.
16. 2007: Pratibha Patil becomes the first woman President of India.

Gender Discrimination

Discrimination against girls and women in the developing world is a devastating reality. It results in millions of individual tragedies, which add up to lost potential for entire economy. There is a direct link between a country's attitude towards women and its progress socially and economically. The status of women is central to the health of a society. If one part suffers, so does the whole.

Tragically, female children are most defenseless against the trauma of gender discrimination. The following obstacles are stark examples of what the females worldwide face. But the new generations of girls represent the most promising source of change for women in the developing world today.

Dowry at the Time of Marriage

In developing countries, the birth of a girl causes great upheaval for poor families. When there is barely enough food to survive, any child puts a strain on a family's resources. But the monetary drain of a daughter feels even more severe, especially in regions where dowry is practised. Dowry is originally intended to help with marriage expenses; dowry came to be seen as payment to the groom's family for taking on the burden of another woman. In some countries,dowries are extravagant, costing years' worth of wages, and often throwing a woman's family into debt. The dowry practice makes the prospect of having a girl even more distasteful to poor families. It also puts young women in danger. A new bride is at the mercy of her in-laws should they decide her dowry is too small. UNICEF estimates that around 5,000 Indian women are killed in dowry related incidents each year.

Neglect of the Girl Child

The developing world is full of poverty-stricken families who see their daughters as an economic predicament. That attitude has resulted in the wide spread neglect of baby girls in Africa. In many communities, it's a regular practice to breastfeed girls for a shorter time than boys so that women can try to get pregnant again with a boy as soon as possible. As a result, girls miss out on life-giving nutrition during a crucial window of their development, which stunts their growth and weakens their resistance to disease. Statistics show that the neglect continues as they grow up. Young girls receive less food, health care and fewer vaccinations overall than boys. Not much changes as they become women. Tradition calls for women to eat last, reduced to picking over the leftovers from men and boys.

Infanticide

In extreme cases, parents make the horrific choice to end their baby girl's life. It is not just poverty but preference for a boy child on religious ground. A daughter is always regarded as liabilities. Sex-selective abortions are even more common than infanticides in India. They are growing ever more frequent as technology makes it simple and cheap to determine a foetus'gender. In Jaipur, it is reported that about 3,500 sex-determined abortions are carried out every year. The gender ratio across India has dropped to an unnatural low of 927 females to 1,000 males due to infanticide and sex-based abortions.

Abuses in the Family

After infancy, the threat of physical harm follows girls throughout their lives. Women in every society are vulnerable to different types of abuse. But the threat is more severe for girls and women who live in societies where women's rights mean practically nothing. Mothers who lack their own rights have little protection to offer their daughters, much less themselves, from male relatives and other authority figures. The frequency of rape and violent attacks against women is alarming. Not only in India,areas of Asia, the Middle East and even Europe, all responsibilities for sexual misconduct falls, by default, to women.

Household Work

School might be an option for a few years,but most girls are pulled out at the age of nine or ten when they're useful enough to work all day at home. Nine million more girls than boys miss out on school every year, according to the UNICEF report. While their brothers continue to go to classes or pursue their hobbies and play, they join the women to do the bulk of the house work. House work consists of continuous, difficult physical labour. A girl is likely to work from before daybreak until the light drains away. She walks barefoot long distances several times a day carrying heavy buckets of water, most likely polluted, just to keep her family alive. She cleans, grinds corn, gathers fuel, tends to the fields, bathes her younger siblings, and prepares meals until she sits down to her own after all the men in the family have eaten.

Most families can't afford modern appliances, so her tasks must be done by hand-crushing corn into meal with heavy rocks, scrubbing laundry against rough stones, kneading bread and cooking gruel over a blistering open fire. There is no time left in the day to learn to read and write or to play with friends. She collapses exhausted each night, ready to wake up the next morning to start another long workday. Most of this labour in the household is performed without recognition. The UN statistics shows that although women produce half the world's food, they own only one per cent of its farmland. In most African and Asian countries including India, women's work is not even considered real labour. Should a woman take a job, she is expected to keep up all her responsibilities at home in addition to her new ones, with no extra help. Women's labour goes overlooked, even though it is crucial to the survival of the family.

Sex Trafficking

Parents send their daughters to a nearby town or city to get jobs that usually involve hard labour and little play. That desperate need for income leaves girls easy prey to sex traffickers and they become sex workers in the illegal industry. Girls who are forced into prostitution to support their families often feel their burden deeply. When at sex work, 50 per cent of their parents hated the girl for what she was doing but the other 50 per cent wanted to stay so that she could earn money for the family. It is estimated that one million children around the world are involved in the sex trade; a third of all sex workers in South-East Asia are between ages of 12 and 17.

Women and Economic Development

Women constitutes about half of society's population. Therefore, the economic development of a country is not possible without the development of the vast segment. Women's participation in economic activity is very important for their own personal development and for the improvement of their status in the society. Women represent thirty per cent of world's official workforce, work for sixty per cent of all the working hours, but receive ten per cent of world's income and own less than one per cent of the world's property.

Women share multiple responsibilities and perform important roles as a producer of food, managers of internal resources, earners of income and as care takers of household affairs. They play vital role in shaping the destiny of the future generation. In spite of all these women in general face different types of discrimination, of which gender discrimination is the most important one.

In India, women suffer many disadvantages as compared to men in terms of literacy rates, labour participation rate and contributing to family income. Women in general and poor rural women in particular are relatively powerless in respect of resources and are marginalized in decision-making process. The Constitution of India no doubt guarantees equality status for women but there still exists a wide gap between the goals prescribed in the Constitution, legislation, policies, plans, programmes and related mechanism, on one hand and situational reality of the status of women on the other.

Emancipation of women is one of the indicators of economic development and the social change. After independence, in the 20th Century, the position of women has changed considerably not only in the sphere of marriage and family responsibility but also in the sphere of education, employment and political activities. However, the women folk in general have not yet attained equal status with men in the society.

Protecting the Women

Women's rights and issues have always been a subject of serious concern of academicians, intelligentia and policymakers. The continuity of changes in socio-economic and psycho-cultural aspects of human living has influenced the role of women. With the process of industrialization, modernization and globalization showing its deep impact on the human society all over the world, the role and responsibilities. In the background of the gigantic transformation, the core issue, which still remains unanswered, is that of women's right and empowerment.

In India patriarchal structure of the society over centuries has gradually led to gender inequality. Women rights in this context have assumed exclusivity. Women are not considered equal to the men in the social context hence the question of women rights arise. The women rights are the means by which a dignified living is ensured thereby safeguarding her rights and virtues. Empowerment of women can be divided into two factors:

- One, the basic fundamental rights of speech, freedom and decision-making are her basic rights as an individual and citizen.
- Two, the right for education and employment are significant for women development and also national development in the wider sense.

The power and freedom to exercise these rights is women empowerment. Women rights and empowerment are not independent of each other. The women empowerment can only be facilitated only if she is able to exercise her rights in the socio-economic spheres of decision-making.

Efforts of the State

Political Empowerment

The principle of gender equality is enshrined in the Constitution of India, in the preamble and fundamental rights, where by the Constitution upholds and grants the equality to women. Among numerous Acts and specific programmes and number of amendments to the Indian Constitution, the 73rd and 74th Amendments of Constitution of India in 1993 are landmarks to ensure political empowerment of women.

The ratification by the Government of India of various International Conventions like Convention on Elimination of All Forms of Discrimination against Women (CEDAW) in 1993,. speaks of the political will. The endorsement by the government of various declarations consolidates the administrative willingness. The description of such provisions incorporates the perception of absolute women empowerment.

The National Commission for Women was set-up in 1990 through an Act of Parliament to safeguard the rights a legal entitlements of women, is considered to be the apex body to ensure and protect rights and work towards the women empowerment.

Social Empowerment

The Constitution surely ensures the legal protection of women's rights, but socio-economic rights of freedom and decision-making is still not realized in spite of several legislative measures by the Central and State Governments to the extent of social empowerment required for women. Some of the important bottlenecks which hamper social empowerment, among others,are as follows:

The rigid patriarchal structure of the Indian Society.

1. The rate of illiteracy among women hampers the awareness and the claims of such provisions.
2. The distinct socialization of girls from the beginning also contribute to the easy acceptance of suppression by women.

The changing trends of education and employment among women have relatively transformed the situation towards the positive direction. But on the other hand the nature of problem has also changed its direction in the sense that crime against women in the working places are at steeply rising.

National Policy 2001

National policy for the empowerment of women is a milestone in ensuring women's rights and facilitates women empowerment. The goal of the national policy is to bring about the advancement, development and empowerment of women in the country. Some of the specific objectives of this policy are:

- Creating an environment through positive economic and social policies for full development of women to enable them to realize their full potential,
- Equal access to health care, quality education at all levels, career and vocational guidance, etc.
- Elimination of discrimination and all forms of violence against women and girl child.

Economic Empowerment

The national policy also provides for economic empowerment through poverty eradication micro-credit programmes, training of women, to facilitate them in playing efficient role in agriculture and industry. The social empowerment of women is facilitated through effective provisions of education, health, nutrition, drinking water and sanitation, gender sensitization, etc. Elimination of all forms of violence against women, whether at domestic or societal levels, including those arising from customs, traditions and accepted practices. A National Resource Centre for Women (NCRW) is being set up which will provide relevant technical back-up for the successful implementation of the policy.

The government has also committed the following provisions to ensure women's rights and women empowerment. Some of the commitments are:

- To increase the investment in education to six per cent of the GDP with major focus on women and the girl child.
- Universalisation of mother and child care programme to reach out to every corner of the country.
- Appointment of commissioner for women's rights.
- National level mechanism for platform for action.

Urban Approach

Women rights and women empowerment are most of the times looked from an urban perspective whereby the situation relatively appears to be in favour of women when compared to their rural counterparts. The rural and tribal women owing to topographical, socio-economic and cultural factors remained away from the government programmes and projects to avail the benefits provided through different agencies both governmental and non-government agencies.

Planned Efforts for Women

Women's development and empowerment was mainly commenced as welfare-oriented programmes in India by the government after independence. Even though there were attempts by the government during the British rule and also many voluntary organisations in the country took the activities for the development of women's status in the society and provided help in educating them, only after independence of India the government tried in a systematic manner to develop the women of the country.

The Government of India introduced the Five Year Planning method to accelerate the development process of the economy and adopted mixed economic system, the mid-way approach, tilting to neither socialist economic approach nor the capitalist market approach.

The Planning Commission was established in the year 1950 under the able guidance and chairmanship of Jawaharlal Nehru, the first Prime Minister of independent India and prepared First Five Year Plan which was introduced in the year 1951. The plan document is an overall development draft of the economy in which provisions also made for the development of women in the economy.

The First Decade of Planning

The two plans implemented in first decade after independence mainly intended to restore the war devastated economy of India after the Second World War. But the planners were aware of the degraded status of the women in the country and made good efforts to provide them equal rights from the beginning of the plan era in the country. The Five Year Plan, 1951-56, provided welfare measures for women and a national body known as the Central Social Welfare Board was set in the year 1953 to implement the welfare programmes for women. Community level womens' groups were set up named as *Mahila Mandal* to mobilise women through the community development movement.

The Second Five Year Plan, 1956-61, introduced measure to improve maternal and child health services including supplementary feeding for children and for nursing mothers. The plan emphasised that women be protected from the injurious work and receive maternity benefits. It also stressed for speedy implementation of the principle of equal pay for equal work and of training provisions to enable women to compete for the higher jobs.

Fifteen Years in Two Plans

In the next two Five Year Plans, the Third Five Year Plan, (1961-66) and the Fourth Five Year Plan, (1969-74) were the eventful years in the political history of India. The boarder conflict with China, battle with Pakistan and death of Jawaharlal Nehru occurred during this period. The National Congress Party which had monopoly in political sphere in the country split after Nehru and his daughter who become Prime Minister of India on the support of left parties' firmly implemented democratic socialism. For three years from 1966-69 planning was suspended and implemented as annual plans and the Fourth Five Year Plan was started only in the year 1969-70. Pakistan's attack on India in 1971 was a very important year in this period when a separate nation called Bangla Desh was established but not before economic upheaval in the economy.

In spite of political and economic crisis, these two plans promoted women's education as an important tool for women's welfare. Women's reproductive health especially emphasis on maternal and child welfare, health education, family planning and nutrition were the focal issues addressed during the Third Five Year Plan. During the Fourth Plan emphasis was given on family planning and mass education of women to reduce the birth rate from 40 to 25 per 1,000. Steps were taken to reduce the high infant and maternal mortality rates through immunisation and supplementary feeding of poor children and expectant and nursing mothers.

The Fifth Five Year Plan, 1974-79:

During this plan period there was another upheaval in the political system of the country. Emergency was declared in 1974 and all the fundamental rights guaranteed in the Constitution of India to the citizens were suspended. However, the general election in 1977 restored the democratic system in the country. But the Congress Party which was the only political party in the country that ruled at Centre since independence was dethroned and a coalition of political parties known as Janata Dal came to power. The Dal government suspended the plan in the middle and tried to redraft it according to their policy framework. Unfortunately that government could not sustained more than three years and in 1979-80 with the coming up of new Congress Government the earlier strategy of planning process was restored.

Nevertheless, during the plan there was an important shift in the approach to women's development, from welfare to development, to cope up with several problems of the family and role of women. The plan emphasised the training of the women through income generation and functional literacy programme. This period witnessed the growth of many women groups working on various gender issues reflected in National Plan of Action 1976. In terms of Five Year Plans the Fifth Five Year plan is considered to be very crucial from the point of view of women development which declared 1975 as International Year of Women.

Plan Efforts in Eighties

The two plans, that Sixth and Seventh Five Year Plan, that were executed in the 1980s of the last century was an eventful decade internationally and nationally. The 70-year-old communist experiment in Russia gradually came to an end by the end of the decade. In India towards the end of the decade there was economic crisis, with the shortage of foreign exchange and two digit inflation in the economy. And economist started doubting the viability of mixed economic experiment after fall of the communist economy.

The Sixth Plan (1980-85) made a landmark in the history of women's development by including a separate chapter on the plan document and adopting a multidisciplinary approach with three thrust on (a) education, (b) health, and (c) employment of women. The plan aimed at women's development through economic independence, educational advance and better access to health care and family planning. The Seventh Five Year Plan (1986-91) targeted women with the concept of equity and empowerment propagated globally by the United Nations' Decade for Women. A significant step in this direction was to identify and promote beneficiary-oriented programmes for women in different developmental sectors which intended direct benefits to women.

Restoration of Full Market Economy

The last decade of the 20th Century was a significant decade for the Indian economy. The public sector dominated mixed economy introduced by Jawaharlal Nehru after the independence of India was abandoned with the adaptation of New Economic Policy in 1991. The Eighth and Ninth Plans were executed in the final decade of the 20th Century and successful in accelerating the growth process which was not achieved under the controlled economy in the earlier decades.

The Eight Five Year Plan (1992-97) launched in 1992 made a shift from development to empowerment approach. It assured the benefits of development in the different sectors would be passing on to women and women should be enabled to function as equal partners to participate in the developmental process. It directed both the Centre and the States to adopt a special strategy for Women's Component Plan (WCP) through which not less than 30 per cent of funds flow to women from all developmental sectors.

In the Ninth Five Year Plan (1997-2002) some major steps towards the gender justice and empowerment of women had been taken.

1. The approach of the plan was to create an environment where women could freely exercise their rights both within and outside the home as equal partners along with men.
2. This plan was an attempt at the convergence of the existing services, resources, infrastructure and manpower available in both women specific and women related sectors.
3. It had suggested for a special vigil on the flow of the earmarked funds for the benefit of women through an effective mechanism to ensure the proposed strategy brought further a comprehensive approach towards empowering women.
4. The Ninth Plan also recommends the adoption of National Policy for the empowerment of women along with a well-defined Gender Development Index for the monitoring and evaluation of women's rights and empowerment

Gender Budgeting

Gender is culturally and socially constructed roles, responsibilities, privileges, relations and expectations of women and men, boys and girls. Because these are socially constructed, they can change overtime and differ from one place to another. Government needs to think both gender and sex when making policies and allocating budget to implement the policies.

A gender responsive budget is a budget that acknowledges the gender partners in the society and allocates money to implement policies and programmes that moves towards a more gender equal society. Gender budgeting is a tool for aollocating resources for women empowerment. It is an application of gender mainstreaming in the budgetary process. It restructures revenues and expenditure in order to promote gender equality.

The concept of gender budgeting was discussed in the 4th UN conference on women at Berjing in 1995. Australia's women's budget was the first attempt to transform public budget into vehicle for gender equality.

For effective gender budgeting two key principles, i.e., (I) political will, and (II) transparency and participation is important.

The Government of India has taken following decisions in order to make gender budgeting more sensitizing.

(i) All departments to open Gender Budget cells

(ii) All departments to reflect benefit-incidence analysis of expenditure.

(iii) Public resources should be distributed in an equitable manner.

Women in 21st Century

The Tenth Five-Year Plan (2002-07) is the first plan of the 21st Century indicating faster economic growth and strengthening of the Indian economy in comparison to developed economies of the world. The Tenth Plan adopted a sector specific strategy for empowerment of women based on the transcription of National Policy for Empowerment of Women to ensure (a) survival, (b) protection, and (c) development of women and children. During the plan four additional strategies have been added.

1. To improve the nutritional and health status of children below the age of six years.
2. To reduce the incidence of infant and child mortality and malnutrition.
3. To ensure that funds/benefits are earmarked for women in all women related sectors.
4. To include an identifiable women component plan in all sectoral programmes of development to ensure that the benefits reach the women.

The last half-century of economic development efforts in India uplifted the women of the country in all spheres of the society and placed at a higher position but still a long way to go in the comparative economy.

✲✲✲

Chapter 2

EDUCATION OF WOMEN

Education is an important determinant of the status of women in the society. Gender inequality in education directly affects economic growth by lowering the average level of human capital. In addition growth is indirectly affected through the impact of gender inequality on investment and population growth. The status and growth of education in a society indicates the socio-economic development. Among others it indicates the (1) development of art and literature, (2) growth of science and technology, and also (3) level of economic development.

Education plays very important role in social and cultural life of a nation. Education has been given importance in India from the ancient times. Indian civilisation is one of the most ancient civilisations, which developed not only good books in prose and poetry but also books on various subjects and good amount of scientific literature. There is a great deal of evidence in Vedic literature, right from the Rig Veda onwards, about the status of women's education. Though the Vedas do not specifically mention whether women were entitled to a life of *brahmacharya* and education during the first twenty-five years of their lives, but there are several references about the education of the girls, especially those belonging to the higher castes, who were receiving extensive education under the able guidance of teachers. Manu in his famous *Manusmriti* states that women needed to acquire education for (1) running a good household, (2) controlling the home economy, (3) inculcating the knowledge of medicine required for infants and household members, and (4) maintain the household crafts. Manu's observation is still relevant in 21st Century.

Proper emphasis was given on education, throughout the period of Hindu supremacy over India, which was continued also during Muslim times. Female education was very much a question of class and most women belonging to the ruling class, aristocracy and even the merchant class could read and write. While Hindus continued their system of educating the girls within the family, many Muslim *madrasas*, set-up by the Muslim rulers attached to the mosques, had both girl and boy students up to the primary level. The situation deteriorated sharply from the early periods of 18th Century.

During British Rule

British administration in India is divided into two periods: (1) British East India Company Administration from 1757 to 1857, and (2) British Administration directly under British government from 1858 to 1947. After the battle of Plassi in 1757 the British East India Company started acquiring princely states, obtained special rights for collection of revenue and took up local administration along with their company business. Several voluntary religious organisations and social organisations took up the spread of women's education as a mission during that period.

The agents who were took initiative to spread women's education at that time can be divided into three:

(1) Christian and other religious missionaries and philanthropic foreign organisations

(2) Indian social reformers worked through associations or independently, and

(3) The company and the British government.

Christian Missionaries

During the early period of British rule different Christian missionaries from England and other European countries came to India for the spread of Christianity and along with it they sincerely took up social welfare measures and also established schools for boys and girls. They were the first to establish schools on modern British style and become pioneers in spreading girls' education. Many women's associations were set up by the religious organisation. The Young Women's Christian Association was established in Bombay in the year 1875. The Muhammadan Educational Conference set-up a Women's Education Cell in 1876.

Hindu Reformist Organisations

Several Hindu reformist organisations such as the Bramho Samaj and the Arya Samaj intensified their efforts for the promotion of education among girls. Other social service organisations such as the Seva Sadan Society of Bombay, the Arya Mahila Samaj, Mahila Seva Samaj of Mysore made good efforts for the spread of girls education along with other social activities. In early 19th Century some social leaders in their individual capacity made good efforts for social reformation to emancipate the women and provide them education.

The company administration tried to change some traditional social customs and many Englishmen who came as the employees of the company wanted to serve the down trodden people and provide them new look through education.

The company not only tried to institute English type schools but also encouraged regional languages and schools to learn Sanskrit. In those days reformation generally meant emancipation of women from the traditional homework of cooking, house keeping and child bearing.

The company government made many legal provisions daringly to provide rights to the women so that they can participate in the activities of the main stream of the society and pursue education which is denied to them; some of the important enactments for social reform that empowered women are:

1. Sati Abolition Act, 1829: This Act banned forcible burning of the wives after the husbands' death, the system that was very prevalent in the country. Of course in spite of legal restriction even today there are incidents of Sati, but it is very rare.
2. Widow Remarriage Act, 1854: As there was the system of marring the girl-child at the early age when there was the death of the husband the girl was not allowed to remarry. Even though now there is no child marriage (it is still there in some parts of India), but still remarriage is being not accepted in the middle and higher class families.
3. The Special Marriage Act, 1872: This Act allows that the boys and girls can marry at their will by registering their marriage before a magistrate. To-day marriage registration is compulsory along with traditional marriage ceremony. But neither parents nor the marrying couple prefers marriage at the court.

Under British Government

The British Parliament, which took over Indian administration in 1858, was a great challenge to the contemporary educational system in the country. The traditional education institutions simply collapsed. The British emphasis on the setting up of government schools based on the English medium, mainly in urban centres had adverse impact on indigenous village-based school system in the country.

The British set-up the first education commission in 1882 known as Indian Education Commission and popularly called the Hunter Commission. It recommended that the attention of the state should be directed to elementary education and made specific recommendations for the development of women's education:

1. Promotion of female education by giving grants to girls' primary schools on easier terms,
2. Appointing female teachers, and
3. Reducing fees for girl students in all the schools.

The Indian National Congress was established in the year 1885 with an intention of organising political organisation for the attainment of independence from the British rule. The leaders of the independence movement were very keen that universal compulsory education of seven years duration should be given to every child in India. According to Montague-Chelmsford Constitution of India in 1919, the subject education made in charge of Central and Provincial Governments in 1921. The Provincial Governments started giving special attention on the education of women and provision of funds for it. The Sarada Act of 1929 prescribed the minimum age of girls for marriage at 14 years, which to some extent helped the girl to attend school until puberty. In this year the women of India were granted voting right to take part in the election process.

During the freedom movement Mahatma Gandhi formulated a scheme of basic education in 1937, and recommended for the adoption of compulsory primary education by the government. The Indian National Congress set-up the B.G. Kher Committee to go into the detail study of educational system in the country; among others it recommended that the goal of compulsory primary education should be achieved by the year 1960. The committee's recommendation led to the formulation of Article 45 of the Directive Principles of the Indian Constitution where it stated that the "State shall endeavour to provide within a period of ten years from the commencement of this Constitution, for free and compulsory education for all children until they complete the age of fifteen years".

Women's Associations

In the first two decades of the 20th Century women in India were more conscious about their rights and education and several associations were formed. The first women conference of India was held at Bethun College, Kolkata in the year 1906 known as Indian Ladies Conference. Various issues relating to the status of women at home, society and contemporary condition of women's education were discussed. The conference was presided by the Maharani of Baroda. The All-India Muslim Ladies Conference was established in 1914. The Women's Indian association was held at Madras under the presidentship of Annie Besant in the year 1917. On behalf of the Association Sarojinee Naidu led a delegation of women representatives and met Sir Montague, the Secretary of State for India, presented memorandum on the issues of education, health care and voting rights for the women in India.

The All-India Women's Conference (AIWC) was established in the year 1926. It organised 22 local conferences on education in different parts of the country. It organised All-India Conference on Education and Social Reforms at Pune in the year 1927. It set-up the Women's Education Fund in 1929 for promotion of education among girls and women.

After Independence

The Government of India after independence appointed several commissions and committees to promote the cause of women's education.

University Education Commission (1948-49)

The commission realising the importance of women's education recommended creating more educational opportunities for women in a planned manner. Among others it recommended, (a) to overcome prejudices against the study of home economics and home management, (b) Social responsibility should be emphasised on the part of the men in mixed educational institutions, (c) Women teachers should be paid equal salary as male teachers, (d) Separate schools should be established for boys and girls between the ages of thirteen and eighteen but college education may be co-educational.

Secondary Education Commission (1952-53)

The Secondary Commission felt no justification to deal with women's education separately. It states that for boys as well as girls education need to be more closely connected with the home and community. It favoured co-education in primary and at the university level but not in the secondary stage. In the co-educational institutions there should be facilities for special co-curricular activities suitable for the girl students.

National Committee on Women Education (1958-59)

A National Committee on Women's Education was set-up in 1958 under the chairmanship of Durgabai Deshmukh, which is known as Deshmukh Committee. It recommended concentrated attention on the important problem of women and recommended allocation of more resources to provide greater facilities to girls at primary and secondary school levels. The other important recommendations of the Deshmukh Committer are:

1. Setting up of national and state-level councils for the promotion of female education. A resolution to this effect in the National Policy on Education was issued in 1968.
2. Concessions in kind should be given to all girls of parents below certain income level.
3. Start more and more co-educational schools at middle and secondary levels.
4. Free and subsidised transport system should be provided to girls to attend schools.
5. Scholarships and other concessions for the girls to encourage them to take up courses in commerce, engineering, agriculture, etc., at the university stage.
6. Involvement of the services voluntary organisations in women's education.
7. Strong enforcement of compulsory education law by the government.

Committee on Differentiation of Curricula for Boys and Girls (1961)

The committee suggested reforming the traditional concept of inferiority of women in the social system. Hence, it recommended inserting relevant topics about women in the school textbooks. The committee also felt that women teachers should be appointed in boys' schools and male teachers in girls' schools. It also recommended exploring the possibility of more employment of women.

Committee on the Causes for Lack of Public Support for Girls' Education and Enlist Public Cooperation (1963)

The committee made special attention to girls' education in rural areas and gave several recommendations in this regard. It recommended: (a) school improvement conferences should be arranged throughout the states, (b) the local bodies should be made responsible for the provision of school infrastructure, and (c) the number of literacy classes for women in rural areas should be increased.

Education Commission (1964-66)

The commission realised the importance of women education in the country and recommended to accelerate all the measures suggested by the National Committee on Women's Education (1958-59). It stated to start separate schools for girls with scholarships and provide hostel facilities. It recommended establishing research units in the universities to deal with specific problems of women's education.

Committee on the Status of Women (1971-74)

This committee was appointed to examine the constitutional, legal and administrative provisions that are required for the increase of the social status of women. There are no specific recommendations to increase the status of women but stressed to implement the recommendations by the earlier committees and commissions. The main recommendations of the committee are:

1. Coeducation as the general policy at the primary and secondary school levels.
2. Compulsory and free education to all girls up to secondary level.
3. Establishment of mobile schools for the children of nomadic tribes, migrant labour and construction workers.
4. Not less than 50 per cent of the teachers in the girls' schools should be women.

The National Policy on Education (1986)

The national policy on education made good efforts to improve the educational system of the country. It recommended certain basic changes to improve the status of women. The following policies were recommended for implementation to increase the status of women:

(a) Education institutes should take up active programmes to tackle women's predicaments by 1995.

(b) Women teachers and women instructors in adult/non-formal education programmes have to receive special orientation to enable them to play an active role towards women's equality.

(c) Women's participation in vocational, technical and professional education should be emphasised.

(d) Special programmes should be developed by research institutes, voluntary organisations and professional groups of artist to promote self-image and general awareness of women.

(e) Women's education cells should be set-up with adequate supporting staff in the states.

National Perspective Plan for Women's Education (1998-2000)

This plan formulated for the women to participate in the area of social, cultural, economic, political and educational fields. Some of the main recommendations to obtain these objectives in the plan to achieve by the year 2000 are:

(a) Media and various forms of communication have to be regarded to generate awareness among the masses regarding the necessity of educating girls.

(b) There should be 50 per cent reservation for women teachers in elementary schools and they should be provided suitable accommodation.

(c) Schools exclusively meant for girls may be set-up.

(d) The Sabitri Bai Phule Parents Scheme of Maharastra could be adopted to help the girls of poor families in other states at least to make them to complete the elementary education.

(e) Special efforts should be made to bring the tribal girls to the school system.

(f) Thirty per cent of the seats should be reserved for girls in apprenticeship training courses on non-transferable basis.

(g) Special scholarships for girls opting for science classes at secondary and higher levels.

(h) More colleges and polytechnic for girls in rural areas.

(i) Thirty per cent of the seats in the higher study course may be reserved for the rural girl students.

(j) Entrepreneurship development programme should be organised separately for the education of women in the age group of 18-30 years with a minimum of matriculation level of education.

(k) Adult education programmes to provide continuous information flow relating to gender relations.

(l) The growing availability of communication should be directed towards keeping up information flows and portraying positive images of women in non-conventional roles.

(m) Women working in the industries and employed elsewhere should be made literate by the employers by allotting time from the working hours for their children.

(n) Fifty per cent of the seats in pre-service courses in all teachers' training institutes should be reserved for women.

Rate of literacy

There are two important indicators of education. They are: (1) Literacy rate, and (2) Gross Enrolment of students from primary to tertiary level. The first *sine qua non* of any achievement of elementary education can be measured through the literacy rates.

Table 2.1 shows the comparative picture of growth of male and female literacy rates in India.

The male-female combined literacy rate in 1901 was 3.9 per cent, the female literacy rate being only 0.60 per cent. Right up to the 1941 it had increased to 7.30, this was a little less than 50 per cent of the total literacy rate of 16.10. The gender gap works out to be 100 per cent. Over the five Censuses conducted in India since independence, the literacy rate for females has increased from 8.86 to 39.29, which means that only since 1981 the gap is less than 50 per cent.

The growth of male and female literacy during 20th Century is shown graphically in Fig.2.1

Table 2.1

Rate of Literacy in India: 1901-2001

Census Year	*Male*	*Female*	*Total Persons*
1901	9.83	0.60	5.39
1911	10.56	1.05	5.92
1921	12.21	1.81	7.16
1931	15.59	2.93	9.50
1941	24.90	7.30	16.10
1951	27.16	8.86	18.33
1961	40.40	15.34	28.31
1971	45.95	21.97	34.45

1981	56.50	29.85	43.67
1991	64.13	39.29	52.21
2001	75.85	54.16	65.10

Source: Census of India, 2001.

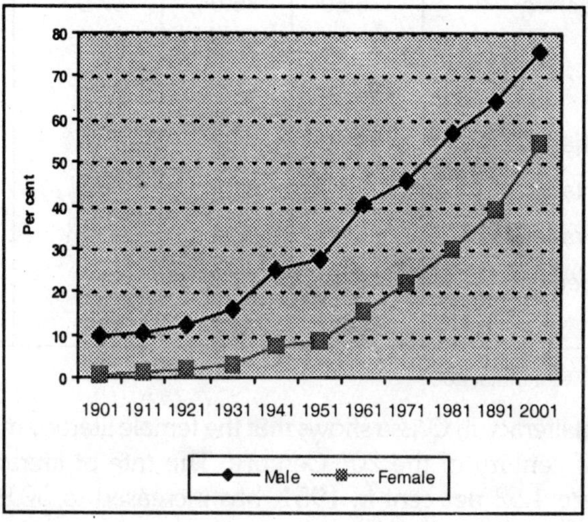

Fig.2.01: Literacy Rates of Male and Females in India: 1901-2001

Literacy in the States

In states the rate of literacy has wide disparity. The state of Kerala is in the top in both male and female literacy rates at 94.2 and 87.7 per cent respectively. Bihar is lowest in the ladder of rate of literacy with 59.7 and 33.1 per cent for male and female respectively. But the gap of percentage difference between male and female literacy is found highest of 31.8 per cent in Rajasthan while Kerala enjoys lowest gap between male and female literacy with 6.6 per cent.

The position of literacy in the states according to the Census of 2001 is presented in Table 2.2.

Table 2.2

Rate of Literacy in the States, 2001

State	***Rate of Literacy***			
	Total	***Male***	***Female***	***Gap between Male-female***
Andhra Pradesh	60.40	70.3	50.4	19.9
Assam	62.95	71.3	54.6	16.7
Bihar	46.40	59.7	33.1	26.6
Gujarat	68.75	79.7	57.8	21.9

Haryana	67.10	78.5	55.7	22.8
Karnataka	66.50	76.1	56.9	19.2
Kerala	90.95	94.2	87.7	6.5
Madhya Pradesh	63.20	76.1	50.3	25.8
Maharashtra	76.50	86.0	67.0	19.0
Orissa	62.95	75.4	50.5	24.9
Punjab	69.30	75.2	63.4	11.8
Rajasthan	59.80	75.7	43.9	31.8
Tamil Nadu	73.35	82.4	64.3	18.1
Uttar Pradesh	55.40	68.6	42.2	26.4
West Bengal	68.30	77.0	59.6	17.4
India	**64.50**	**75.3**	**53.7**	**21.6**

Source: Census of India, 2001

Growth of literacy in Orissa shows that the female literacy made good progress during the half century of the 20th Century. The rate of literacy of the females, which was mere 4.52 per cent in 1951, has increased to 50.97 per cent by the turn of the century. Growth of literacy rate and enrolment of girls in Orissa from the year 1951 to 2001 is presented in Table 2.3.

Table 2.3

Male and Female Literacy Rate in Orissa

Year	***Rate of Literacy Per cent***			***Enrolment of Girls In Million***	
	Male	***Female***	***Total***	***Primary***	***Upper Primary***
1951	27.32	4.52	15.10	0.26	0.08
1961	34.68	8.65	21.66	0.44	0.13
1971	38.29	13.92	26.18	0.53	0.32
1981	46.39	20.60	33.62	0.65	0.48
1991	63.09	34.68	49.09	0.71	0.62
2001	75.4	50.5	62.95	0.71	0.77

Source: Census of India, 2001

Enrolment of Students

Pre-independence Era:

In spite of efforts by the government and private institutions to promote girls' education in the 20th Century up to the independence of India the progress has been very slow. Between 1921-22 and 1946-47 the growth rate of all types of schools showed 20 per cent in 25 years. The percentage of girl students in total number of students in educational institutions formed 16.97 per cent, which increased to 23.58 per cent by 1947-48, that shows a growth rate of 9.49 per cent in a period of quarter century.

Total number of schools in the country and enrolment of boys and girls in those institutions is presented in Table 2.4.

Table 2.4

Number of Educational Institutes and Girl Children

Year	*No.*	*Enrolment of Students*			*Per cent of Girls*
		Boys	*Girls*	*Total*	
1921-22	23517	69.63	14.24	83.87	16.97
1926-27	27756	93.15	18.42	111.57	16.51
1931-32	33969	102.74	24.93	127.67	19.53
1936-37	33898	110.08	31.38	141.46	22.18
1939-40	34564	122.66	37.27	159.93	22.30
1946-47	28196	139.49	42.98	182.47	23.58

Source: Progress of Education in India, Government of India, 1948

Women's education suffered due to limited financial resources as the government provided meagre funds for women's education. Unlike boys education, the girls' education require higher investment among others due to the following reasons:

1. Separate schools for girls.
2. Hostels have to be provided.
3. Escorts have to be appointed to bring the students to school and back, as the girls are not traditionally allowed outdoor for any work in those days.
4. Women teachers have to be trained and appointed, as parents did not allow their daughters in the schools with male teachers.
5. Free scholarships have to be provided as incentive to parents so that they would agree to forego earning and labour of their daughters.

On the eve of independence of India the schools run by different management for the girls shows that the role of the government was lowest with only 3.22 per cent. The private management schools for the girls constitutes first position with 48.28 per cent, of which 6.13 per cent of schools are run by private institutes with out any financial aid from the government. Next to private institutions, quasi-government organisations of District Boards and Municipal Councils are in the second position with 36.61 per cent.

The number of girls' schools managed by different organisation by the year 1946-47 is presented in Table 2.5.

Table 2.5

Girls' Schools Managed by Different Organisations

	1946-47	
Management	***No.***	***Per cent***
Government	908	3.22
District Board	7,856	27.91
Municipal Board	2,453	8.71
Private (aided)	11,863	42.15
Private (unaided)	1,722	6.13
Unrecognised	3,344	11.88
Total	**28,146**	**100**

Source: Progress of Education in India, Government of India, 1948

After Independence:

There has been considerable increase in the number of primary and upper primary level institutions during the period in the country between 1950-51 and 2003-04. This is evident from Table 2.6 below. The number of schools which were a mere 2 lakh in 1950-51 increased to 188.97 crore by the turn of the Century, and by the end of 2003-04 the number of schools sharply increased and reached a figure of 755.90 crore. Over the 54 years from 1950-51 to 2003-04 the growth in the number of primary schools was 240 per cent, at the rate about 4 per cent annually; while growth in upper primary schools and high schools were 1,153 and 1,981 per cent over the period, which shows maximum growth in high schools, on an average of 34 per cent per annum.

Table 2.6

Growth of Secondary Educational Institutions in India 1951-2004

Year	*Primary*	*Upper Primary /M.E.*	*High/Higher Secondary*	*Total schools In Crore*
1950-51	209671	13596	7416	0.02
1955-56	278135	21730	10838	0.03
1960-61	330399	49663	17329	0.04
1965-66	391064	75798	27614	0.09
1970-71	408378	90621	37051	0.18
1975-76	454270	106571	43054	0.36
1980-81	494503	118555	51573	0.73

1985-86	528872	134846	65837	1.47
1990-91	560935	151456	79796	2.95
1991-92	565786	152077	81747	5.90
1992-93	572541	153921	84086	11.81
1993-94	572923	155707	88411	23.62
1994-95	581305	163605	92252	47.24
1996-97	598000	177000	73000	94.48
2001-02	664041	219626	133492	188.97
2002-03	651382	245274	137207	377.95
2003-04	710471	262649	146796	755.90

Source: Government of India, Ministry of HRD, Department of Education, New Delhi.

Table 2.7 Enrolment of students in India presents the progress of sex-wise enrolment in India in absolute figures for different stages of school education from 1950-51 to 2003-04.

Primary Schools (Classes I-V): In 1950-51 the enrolment of girl students was 5.4 million in the country which shoot up to 49.8 million, a pronominal growth of 9 fold increase, by the year 2001. But in comparison to the boys, the girls formed 39 per of boys in 1950-51 that made a good improvement to 50 per cent by 2001.

Middle Schools (Classes VI-VIII): The growth of enrolment in middle schools was commendable. It increased from mere 0.5 million to 17.5 million. At the beginning of the period the girls formed just 19 per cent of the boys but at the end of the period it increased to 69 per cent of the boys, a good achievement.

High School (Classes IX-XII): The combined growth of enrolment of boys and girls in the high schools increased from 1.5 million to 27.6 million. But the growth of girls' enrolment has been very significant. The enrolment increased from 0.2 million to 10.7 million by the end of the period. In the year 1950-51 the enrolment of girl students formed 15 per cent of boys enrolled but in 2004-05 it increased to as high as 69 per cent of the boys.

Table 2.7

Sex-wise Enrolments of Students 1950-51 – 2004-05

Year	Primary (I-V)		Middle/ Upper Primary (VI-VIII)		High/Higher Secondary (IX-XII)		All Total
	Figures in million						
	Boys	Girls	Boys	Girls	Boys	Girls	
1950-51	13.8	5.4	2.6	0.5	1.3	0.2	23.8
1955-56	17.1	7.5	3.8	1.0	2.2	0.4	32.0
1960-61	23.6	11.4	5.1	1.6	2.7	0.7	45.1
1965-66	32.2	18.3	7.7	2.8	4.4	1.3	66.7
1970-71	35.7	21.3	9.4	3.9	4.9	1.7	76.9
1975-76	40.6	25.0	11.0	5.0	6.5	2.4	90.5
1980-81	45.3	28.5	13.9	6.8	7.6	3.2	105.3
1985-86	52.2	35.2	17.7	9.6	11.5	5.0	131.2
1990-91	58.1	41.0	20.9	12.4	14.0	6.9	153.3
1991-92	59.6	42.3	22.0	13.6	13.5	6.9	157.9
1992-93	60.5	34.9	23.7	15.0	15.0	7.7	156.8
1993-94	61.8	46.4	24.2	15.7	15.3	8.0	171.4
1994-95	62.3	46.8	24.5	15.8	16.0	8.4	173.8
1996-97	62.5	47.9	24.7	16.3	17.2	9.8	178.4
1997-98	61.2	47.5	23.7	15.8	17.1	10.2	175.5
1998-99	62.7	48.2	24.0	16.3	17.3	10.5	179.0
1999-00	64.1	49.5	25.1	17.0	17.2	11.0	183.9
2000-01	64.0	49.8	25.3	17.5	16.9	10.7	184.2
2001-02	63.6	50.3	26.1	18.7	18.4	12.1	189.2
2002-03	65.1	59.3	26.3	20.0	19.5	13.7	203.9
2003-04	68.4	59.9	27.3	21.5	20.0	14.4	211.5
2004-05	69.7	61.1	28.5	22.7	21.7	15.4	219.1

Source: Government of India, Ministry of HRD, Department of Education, New Delhi.

The percentage growth of girls' students' enrolment in the three stages of school is presented in Table 2.08. In the three levels of schooling the percentage of enrolment gradually declined from primary to the high school stage. The trend of percentage declining of enrolment of girl students, from primary to high school, in 1950-51 was in this order 28.1→ 16.1→ 13.3 per cent while in the year 1994-95 it was 42.8→ 38.9→ 34.4 per cent. Girls' enrolment in high schools made good progress during the period under study.

Table 2.8

Enrolment of Girl Students Primary to Higher Education: 1950-51 – 2004-05

Figures are in Per cent to Total Enrolment				
Year	**Primary**	**Middle**	**High School**	**Hr. Education**
1950-51	28.1	16.1	13.3	10.0
1955-56	30.5	20.8	15.4	10.6
1960-61	32.6	23.9	20.5	16.0
1965-66	36.2	26.7	22.0	20.4
1970-71	37.4	29.3	25.0	20.0
1975-76	38.1	31.3	26.9	23.2
1980-81	38.6	32.9	29.6	26.7
1985-86	40.3	35.6	30.3	33.0
1990-91	41.5	36.7	32.9	33.3
1991-92	41.9	38.2	33.8	32.3
1992-93	42.6	38.8	33.9	33.2
1993-94	42.7	39.1	34.3	33.5
1994-95	42.8	38.9	34.4	34.0
1995-96	43.1	39.5	36.7	36.0
1996-97	43.2	39.7	36.4	36.7
1997-98	43.5	40.4	36.5	37.5
1998-99	43.9	40.8	37.8	38.8
1999-00	43.6	40.4	38.9	38.7
2000-01	43.7	40.9	38.6	39.4
2001-02	44.1	41.8	39.5	39.9
2002-03	46.8	43.1	39.5	39.9
2003-04	46.7	44.0	41.1	39.7
2004-05	46.7	44.4	41.5	38.9

Source: Government of India, Ministry of HRD, Department of Education, New Delhi.

Gross Enrolment Ratios (GER) in India

The gross enrolment ratio is defined as the percentage of the enrolment in Class I-V and VI-VIII to the estimated child population in the age groups 6-11 years and 11-14 years. Enrolment at primary stage 6-11 years include under age and overage children. Hence, the total percentage may be more than 100. The gross enrolment ratios for the age groups 6-11 years and 11-14 years are presented in Table 2.9.

Table 2.9

Gross Enrolment Ratios in India

Year	Girls			Boys		
	I-V	VI-VIII	I-VII	I-V	VI-VIII	I-VIII
1950-51	24.8	4.6	17.7	60.6	20.6	46.4
1960-61	41.4	11.3	30.9	82.6	33.2	65.2
1970-71	60.5	20.8	44.4	95.5	46.5	75.5
1980-81	64.1	28.6	52.1	95.8	54.3	82.2
1990-91	85.5	47.0	70.8	114.0	76.6	100.0
1994-95	78.2	50.0	68.8	96.6	68.9	87.2
2000-01	85.9	49.9	72.4	104.9	66.7	90.3
2001-02	86.9	52.1	73.6	105.3	67.8	90.7
2002-03	93.1	56.2	79.3	97.5	65.3	85.4
2003-04	95.67	57.69	81.51	100.75	66.87	88.02

Source: Government of India, Ministry of HRD, 2005, Department of Education, New Delhi.

The total enrolment at primary and upper primary school levels in India witnessed a steady increase. During 2000-01 and 2001-02 the growth rate of enrolment for girls at the elementary level was higher than that of boys. Participation of girls at all levels of school education has improved appreciably over the years. The GER at primary and upper primary levels improved in 2001-02 over the previous years. It is increased progressively from 32.1 in 1950-51 to 84.91 in 2003-04 with the rate of increase in GER of girls is higher than that of the boys; the gender gap in enrolment is declining.

Drop-outs in Primary and Middle Schools

Indicative of the positive effect of increasing rates of enrolment there is a visible decline in the drop-out rates between 1961 and 1977 from 64.9 per cent to 38.9 per cent at the primary level, from 78.3 per cent to 52.3 per cent at the middle level. However, the dropout rates in case of girls have always remained higher than that of boys. This was further compounded by the highly pronounced regional and rural-urban differentials, besides sex differentials which continue to persist. Though the gains in the educational status of women have been impressive, gender justice in education still continues to be a distant goal, with 60.7 per cent of women being illiterate as per the 1991 Census. The available data on drop-out rates in Class I-V for the year 1996-97 reveal that the dropout rate for the century as a whole was 38.9 per cent. It was 39.37 per cent among the boys and 38.35 per cent among the girls.

The drop-out figures of boys and girls in the primary and middle schools from the year 1960-61 to 2002-03 is presented in Table 2.10.

Table 2.10

Drop-out Rates at Primary and Middle School Stages

	1960-61	*1970-71*	*1980-81*	*1990-91*	*2001-02*	*2002-03*
Classes I-V						
Boys	61.7	64.5	56.2	40.1	39.03	34.9
Girls	70.9	70.9	62.5	46.0	39.90	33.70
Total	**64.9**	**67.0**	**58.7**	**42.6**	**39.46**	**34.3**
Classes VI-VIII						
Boys	75.0	74.6	88.0	59.1	54.6	52.8
Girls	85.0	83.4	79.4	65.1	56.9	53.5
Total	**78.3**	**77.9**	**72.7**	**60.9**	**55.7**	**53.1**

Source: Government of India, Ministry of HRD, Department of Education, New Delhi.

There were wide inter-state disparities in retention and dropout. Of the estimated population of 205 million in the age group of 6-14 years on March 2001-02, nearly 82.5 per cent was enrolled in schools compared with 82.4 per cent in 2000-01. The student retention at the primary school stage was about 59 per cent (1992-97). At the primary level the drop-out level decreased from 40.7 per cent in 2000-01 to 39.03 per cent in 2001-02. Further, it decreased to 34.9 per cent in 2002-03.

At the upper primary level the drop-out rate increased marginally from 53.7 per cent in 2000-01 to 54.6 per cent in 2001-02. While in 2002-03 the drop-out rate decreased from 54.6 per cent to 52.8 per cent. Though the drop-out at the elementary education stage has declined over the years, it is still relatively high, especially in the case of girl students for whom the rates in 2001-02 were 39.9 per cent and 56.9 per cent at the primary and upper primary levels respectively. While in 2002-03 it further decreased to 33.7 per cent and 53.5 per cent respectively. The drop-out rate at the primary level (classes 1 to 5) declined from 39.0 per cent in 2001-02 to 31.4 per cent in 2003-04. As on October 2005, number of out-of-school children as reported by States Union Territories was down to 95 lakh from 320 lakh in 2001.

Apart from the availability or access to primary school within a walking distance of habitations, there are a number of other problems, which are required to be tackled on an urgent basis. Some of these are low enrolment of girls, high drop-out rates, education of disadvantaged groups, lack of physical infrastructure like school buildings, teachers, teaching and learning equipment and the problem of working children low level of achievement and regional disparities.

Mahila Samakhya

Mahila Samakhya Scheme was introduced in 1989 for the education and empowerment of women in rural areas. It fouses on (a) enabling greer acces women for education, (b) generating demand for education, (c) building capabilities and strengthening women's abilities, and (d) active participation of women in the process of educational development. This scheme now covers nine states of Andhra Pradesh, Assam, Bihar, Gujarat, Jharkhand, Karnataka, Kerala, Uttar Pradesh and Uttaranchal spread in 59 districts reaching more than 12,000 vilages in the country.

Higher Education for Women

In order to facilitate better access to women in universities, the UGC runs a scheme for funding women's hostels. The faculty-wise distribution of enrolment of women in higher education in the Eighth Plan shows that at the undergraduate level, the percentage of women in arts, sciences and commerce rose from 34.7 per cent in 1990-91 to 37.4 per cent in 1996-97. In engineering and architecture, it increased from 10.9 per cent to 14.9 per cent and in medicine, from 34.3 per cent to 35.4 per cent. In the doctorate and post-doctoral stage, there was an increase in the number of women from 26.2 to 29.2 per cent of total students. In 1999-2000, women accounted for 34.1 per cent of the total enrolment. To sum up, despite some clear-cut gains of women's participation in higher education, a big gender gap still exists. This is shown in Table 2.11.

There has been further impressive growth in the area of higher education with an increase in the student enrolment in higher education from 7.26 million in 1997-98 to 9.95 million in 2003-04. Enrolment of women students rose to 3.81 million constituting 40 per cent of the total in 2003-04 and 4.03 million in 2004-05 constituting 40.22 per cent of the total enrolment. There has also been a significant increase in the student enrolment under open and distance education system.

The priority for the 10th Plan is on the expansion of education mainly in the unreserved areas with a focus on improving the coverage of women and the disadvantaged groups, using financial assistance as a leverage to secure better performance of the system, updating of the syllabi to enhance their relevance, improvement in the internal resource generation and implementation of a model code of governance to reduce non-academic influence in the higher education system.

Table 2.11

Enrolment of Girls at Higher Education, 1990-91 – 1996-97

Level of Education	*1990-91*			*1996-97*		
	Girls	*Per cent*	*Total*	*Girls*	*Per cent*	*Total*
Graduate (B.A./B.Sc./B.Com.)	11.40	(34.7)	32.87	18.20	(37.4)	48.72
Postgraduate (M.A./M.Sc./M.Com.)	1.16	(32.8)	3.54	1.65	(30.5)	5.41
B.Ed./B.T.	0.40	(44.2)	0.92	0.50	(43.1)	1.16
B.E./B.Arch.	0.26	(10.9)	2.41	0.49	(14.9)	3.28
M.B.B.S.	0.28	(34.3)	0.84	0.43	(35.4)	1.21
Ph.D./D.Sc./ D.Phil.	0.10	(26.2)	0.33	0.12	(29.2)	0.41
Total	**13.60**	**(33.2)**	**40.91**	**21.39**	**(35.5)**	**60.19**

Source: Government of India, Ministry of HRD, Department of Education, New Delhi.

Education of Women in the States

The gender gap in literacy index of 15 major states of India for the year 2001 is presented in Table 2.12.

The rate of literacy is higher among males in the states while literacy Index is higher with the females in comparison to the males. Kerala tops in Literacy Index for both male and female and Bihar has lowest index in both male and female. In four states male index is lower to Indian figures while in seven states female index is below the national figures, which includes, Andhra Pradesh, Madhya Pradesh, Orissa, Assam, Bihar, Rajasthan and Uttar Pradesh.

Table 2.12

Literacy Index in Major States of India, 2001

State	*Total ALI*	*Male ALI*	*Female ALI*
Andhra Pradesh	0.703	0.504	0.604
Assam	0.713	0.546	0.630
Bihar	0.597	0.331	0.464
Gujarat	0.797	0.578	0.688
Haryana	0.785	0.557	0.671
Karnataka	0.761	0.569	0.665
Kerala	0.942	0.877	0.910
MP	0.761	0.503	0.632

Maharashtra	0.860	0.670	0.765
Orissa	0.754	0.505	0.630
Punjab	0.752	0.634	0.693
Rajasthan	0.757	0.439	0.598
Tami Nadu	0.824	0.643	0.734
Uttar Pradesh	0.686	0.422	0.554
West Bengal	0.770	0.596	0.683
India	**0.753**	**0.537**	**0.645**

Note: Following the measure of UNDP, the index numbers have been constructed.

Source: Census Report, 2001, Govt. of India.

The GER in the States

The GER is highest in Gujarat which is 102.91 and is lowest in Bihar with 60.77. In the enrolment of boys Gujarat is again commands highest position, while Maharashtra tops in the enrolment of girls. The gender gap in enrolment is highest in Rajasthan. The only state where the enrolment of girls exceeds boys is Punjab. The gross enrolment ratios of the states are presented in Table 2.13.

Table 2.13

Gross Enrolment Ratio in the States, 2001

State	*Total*	*Boys*	*Girls*	*Gap*
AP	81.84	84.28	79.4	4.88
Assam	99.35	108.25	90.44	17.81
Bihar	60.77	75.92	45.62	30.3
Gujarat	102.91	112.84	92.98	19.86
Haryana	73.10	73.58	72.61	0.97
Karnataka	98.37	101.76	94.97	6.79
Kerala	91.00	92.32	89.68	2.64
MP	91.54	101.71	81.36	20.35
Maharashtra	100.97	104.23	97.71	6.52
Orissa	90.31	105.52	75.1	30.42
Punjab	73.78	73.45	74.1	-0.65
Rajasthan	87.77	105.28	70.25	35.03
TN	95.00	95.47	94.53	0.94
UP	54.24	67.57	40.9	26.67
WB	85.91	91.06	80.75	10.31
India	**81.31**	**90.26**	**72.36**	**17.9**

Source: Selected Educational Statistics, 2000-01, Ministry of Human Resource Development, Govt. of India.

Comparison of three types of indices, namely, Adult Literacy. General Enrolment of Students and Educational Index provide different pictures in the states. The indices are presented in Table 2.14. In adult literacy and Education Index males in Kerala occupies first position, but in enrolment of boy students Gujarat is at the top of the index figure among the states. Bihar is at the lowest level both in literacy index as well as educational Index while U P is in the lowest position in Gross Enrolment index among the states.

Table 2.14

Indices of Literacy, Enrolment and Education in the States – 2001

State	*Male*			*Female*		
Index->	*ALI*	*GERI*	*EI*	*ALI*	*GERI*	*EI*
AP	0.703	0.843	0.750	0.504	0.843	0.617
Assam	0.713	1.083	0.836	0.546	1.083	0.725
Bihar	0.597	0.759	0.651	0.331	0.759	0.474
Gujarat	0.797	1.128	0.907	0.578	1.128	0.761
Haryana	0.785	0.736	0.769	0.557	0.736	0.617
Karnataka	0.761	1.018	0.847	0.569	1.018	0.719
Kerala	0.942	0.923	0.936	0.877	0.923	0.892
MP	0.761	1.017	0.846	0.503	1.017	0.674
Maharashtra	0.860	1.042	0.921	0.670	1.042	0.794
Orissa	0.754	1.055	0.854	0.505	1.055	0.688
Punjab	0.752	0.735	0.746	0.634	0.735	0.668
Rajasthan	0.757	1.053	0.856	0.439	1.053	0.644
T N	0.824	0.955	0.868	0.643	0.955	0.747
U P	0.686	0.676	0.683	0.422	0.676	0.507
W B	0.770	0.911	0.817	0.596	0.911	0.701
India	**0.753**	**0.903**	**0.803**	**0.537**	**0.903**	**0.659**

Source: Compiled by the author

In case of females' literacy and Education Index again Kerala is at the top and UP is at the lowest position. In the enrolment of girls in the schools Gujarat tops with index of 1.128 and the last position goes to UP where the gross enrolment index is computed at 0.676. Bihar is having lowest educational index in India with the index of 0.474 as against 0.892 for Kerala.

National Educational Policy

In the Indian Constitution, school education was included in the state list. As such it was responsibility of the state governments to provide elementary education to all between the age group of 6-14 years. At the policy level the situation changed with constitutional changes made in 1976 by which school education was put in the concurrent list. Universalisation of elementary education became a shared responsibility of the Central and the State Government. The national government realized its direct responsibility in this field after the adoption of national policy on education in 1986.

The government has taken many steps for the growth of elementary education and there has been a significant progress over the past 50 years. In 1950-51 when the plan era commenced, 83.4 per cent of people were illiterate and it is now 53.25 per cent according to 2001 Census. The enrolment at primary level increased more than five times and secondary level by about 15 times. Though the achievements are commendable, the quantum of the unfinished agenda makes the education scheme very pathetic. India development report 1999-00 observed that fifty years after independence, the slow progress of education particularly primary education in India is a matter of deep shame. India holds the world record for the number of illiterate persons.

National Programme for Education of Girls (NPEG)

In July 2003, Government of India approved a new programme called National Programme for Education of Girls at elementary level (NPEG) as an amendment to the existing scheme of *Sarva Sikshya Abhiyan* (SAA) for providing additional support for education of underprivileged/disadvantaged girls at the elementary level. The scheme is implemented in Educationally Backward Blocks (EBBs), where the level of female literacy is low and the gender gap is above the national average; in blocks of the districts which are not covered under EBBs but have at least 5 per cent SC/ST population and where SC/ST female literacy is below 10 per cent and also in select urban slums. The NEPG has adopted these objectives to develop girls' education in the rural sector:

- To develop a model girl-child friendly school at the cluster level,
- To provide additional incentives such as stationer, slates, workbooks and uniform.
- Additional interventions like awards to schools/teachers, student evaluation, bridge courses and learning through open schools.
- Teachers training and child care centres at the cluster level but expenses not exceeding Rs.60,000 per annum.

Kasturba Gandhi Balika Vidyalaya

A new scheme called *Kasturba Gandhi Balika Vidyalaya* (KGBV) has been approved for launching during 2004-05 for setting up 750 residential schools with boarding facilities at elementary level for girls belonging predominantly to the SC, ST, other backward castes (OBC) and minorities in different areas. A provision of Rs. 489 crore has been made for the year 2004-05. So far 525

KGBVs have been approved by the Department of Elementary Education involving an amount of Rs. 123.03 crore for 2004-05.

Primary Education Fund

A separate, dedicated, non-lapsable fund has been created as *Prathamik Shikshya Kosh*, which is maintained by the Ministry of HRD, Department of Elementary Education and Literacy. An educational cess of 2 per cent on all direct and indirect Central taxes has been imposed through the Finance (No. 2) Act, 2004. The proceeds would be available on a rollover basis for the schemes of basic education and the mid-day meal scheme. Budget provision for the mid-day meal scheme during 2004-05 is Rs. 1,675 crore. In addition Rs. 1,232 crore has been provided to the States/Union Territories as Additional Central Assistance (ACA) under state sector as earmarked outlay for meeting cooking cost.

The objective of the *Kosh* is to provide additional support to the education of girls at the elementary level through the following additional initiatives:

(1) To develop a school as a model girl-child friendly school, at the cluster level.

(2) To provide additional incentives such as stationary, slates, workbooks and uniforms and to meet any other locally-felt need within the existing ceiling of Rs. 150 per child per annum.

(3) Learning through open schools, teacher training and childcare centres at the cluster level within a ceiling of Rs. 60,000 per annum.

(4) Additional interventions like awards to schools/teachers, student evaluation, remedial teaching, bridge courses, alternative schools,

(5) Mobilisation and community monitoring within a ceiling of Rs. 95,000 per cluster over a five-year period.

(6) Development of materials

(7) Planning, training and management support.

Although impressive strides have been made with regard to development of education of women, at the same time it is to be stated here that the present educational system cannot help to solve all problems faced by the women in India. We must develop a value-based education system, which can aware the women of her duties and rights. She has to be allowed the full expression of her potential, so that women can be dynamic partners in the building of new India.

National Agenda for Governance (NAG)

Having realized fully the gravity of the problem, the National Agenda for Governance (NAG) has assigned highest priority for education and come out with concrete measures. The following are the specific agenda for action.

- Free and compulsory primary education for all up to 5th standard and total eradication of illiteracy.
- Education of prioritized groups, girls SC/STs and backward classes and educationally backward minorities.
- Access quality and equal opportunity for all up to school stage.
- Improvement of quality at all levels.
- Increase in government and non-government spending on education and bringing this up to six per cent of GDP level.

The Directive Principle of Constitution

India's commitment to the spread of knowledge and freedom of thought among its citizens is reflected in its constitution. The Directive Principles contained in article 45 enjoins that "the state shall endeavour to provide within a period of ten years from the commencement of this Constitution for free and compulsory education for all children until they complete the age of fourteen years". Article 29(I) provides that any citizen having a distinct language script, special care of the economic and the educational interests of the underprivileged sections, particularly the scheduled castes and scheduled tribes is laid down as an obligation of the state under Article 46. Though education is in the concurrent list of the Constitution, the state government plays a very major role in the development of education particularly in the primary and secondary education.

The 73rd and 74th Constitutional Amendments provide for decentralization of the activities and facilitate transfer of power and participation of the local self-government bodies or the Panchayati Raj Institutions. It has created a congenial ambience for the PRIs to play a more dynamic and proactive role. States are expected to evolve institutional arrangements both in rural and urban areas for undertaking these activities. These structures have been providing voice to women, schedule castes/tribes, minorities and parents and educational functionaries. They have also been delegated responsibilities with regard to location and relocation of existing primary and upper primary schools on the basis of micro-planning and schools mapping. In this regard, decentralization of school management to grassroots level bodies is an important policy initiative.

Universal Elementary Education (UEE)

The first major international affirmation on education for all was at the world conference on education in Jomtein (Thailand) in 1990 when 155 countries including India and 155 organisations resolved to universalize primary education and significantly reduce illiteracy before 2000. The conference adopted the vision that all children have the fundamental human right to basic education. Latter the world education forum at Dakar, Senegal 2000, 164 countries including India reaffirmed the goal of education for all, as laid out at the Jomtein and other international conferences. It urged government to achieve quality basic education for all by 2015 or earlier with emphasis on girls' education. This was followed by the UN millennium development goal 2000, which binds countries to ensure that all children everywhere complete primary schooling by 2015.

To achieve universal elementary education a number of schemes and programme were launched over the past 55 years, especially after the Constitutional Amendment in 1976.

Some of the major schemes initiated were:

1. The non-formal education 1977 later revised a education guarantee scheme and alternative and innovative education in 2000 for targeting out of school children.
2. Operation blackboard 1987 for improving human and physical resource in school, teacher education scheme 1987,
3. For teacher training and providing academic support,
4. Mid-day meal scheme 1995 to enhance nutritional status of students,
5. The DPEP 1994 for achieving universal primary education, and
6. The UNICEF assisted janashala programme 1998 for community participation in schools.

Programmes on Elementary Education

From the year 1987 to 2003 ten specific schemes were introduced in the country for the development of education, namely: (1) operation blackboard (OBB), (2) District Primary Education Programme (DPEP), (3) Non-formal education (NFE), (4) National Programme of Nutritional Support to Primary Education (Mid-day Meal Scheme), (5) Teachers Education, (6) Total Literacy Campaign (TLC), (7) Community Polytechnics, (8) Siksha Karmi Project (SKP) (9) Area Intensive Programme for Educationally Backward Minorities, and (10) Integrated Education for Disabled Children.

Launching of six of these projects and year of launching is presented in Table 2.15.

Table: 2.15

Programme on Elementary Education

No.	*Programmes*	*Launching Year*
1	Operation Blackboard	1987
2	DPEP	1994
3	Mid-day Meal Scheme	1995
4	NLM	1998
5	SSA	2001-02
6	NPEG/KGPV	2003

Source: Compiled by the author

(A) Operation Blackboard (OBB):

One of the schemes, operation blackboard was started in 1987. It is aimed at improving the school climate and enhancing retention and learning achievement of children by providing certain minimum essential facilities in all primary schools. The scheme has brought about remarkable qualitative and quantitative improvement in primary education. More than 5,23,000 primary schools have already been all over the country under this scheme. These schools have been provided with central assistance.

Government has taken steps for providing basic infrastructure including school buildings under the operation blackboard scheme in rural areas since 1990-91. During the period from 1991-92 to 2002-03, 12421 primary school buildings were constructed involving an expenditure of Rs. 175.12 crore. During 2003-04, 47 school buildings have been completed under OBB involving an expenditure of Rs. 0.28 crore.

(B) District Primary Education Programme (DPEP)

This programme launched in 1994, is conceived as a beachhead overhauling the primary education system in India. The programme aims to operate the strategies for achieving UEE through district specific planning and disaggregated target setting. It draws upon the accumulated national experience of several state level initiatives that were started earlier. It moves away from the schematic piecemeal approach of the earlier programme and takes a holistic view of primary education with emphasis on decentralized management community mobilization and district specific planning based on contextually and research-based inputs.

Basic Objectives of DPEP are:

1. To provide all children with access to primary education either in the formal system or through the non-formal education (NFE) programme.
2. To reduce differences in enrolment drop-out rates and learning achievement among gender and social groups to less than 5 per cent.
3. To reduce overall primary drop-out rates for all students to les than 10 per cent.
4. To raise average achievement levels by at least 25 per cent over measured base line levels and ensuring. Achievements of basic literacy and numeric competencies and a minimum of 40 per cent achievement levels in other competencies by all primary school children.

The Government of India finances 85 per cent of the project cost as a grant to the DPEP state implementation societies and the concerned state government provide the rest. External funding resource the Central Governments share. The IDA has approved credit amounting $260 million and $425 million under phase-i and phase-ii respectively. The European Union (EU) is providing a grant of 150 million ECU. The ODA UK is extending a grant of $80.21 million. The grant from the Netherlands amounts to $25.8 million.

The DPEP in States

The first phase of the programme was launched in 42 districts of the states of Assam, Haryana, Karnataka, Kerala, Maharashtra, Tamil Nadu and Madhya Pradesh. In the second phase the programme has been launched in 30 districts of Orissa. Himachal Pradesh, Andhra Pradesh, West Bengal, Uttar Pradesh and Gujarat are included in he first phase. The DPEP has been able to set-up project management structures at district, state and national levels, create the environment and capacity for micro-planning, take up the challenge of pedagogical innovation, create a responsive institutional base which includes both government and non-government institutions enhance community participation and strengthen the process of catering to special focus groups such as tribal, scheduled castes, women and other marginalized sections.

The DPEP has made a decisive impact on increasing enrolment, reducing repetition rates and improving classroom processes. While the DPEP has been targeting backward districts with female literacy below the national average and where TLCs have stirred up a demand for elementary education several state level initiatives have shown tremendous potential. These are directed at improving literacy levels in the five low literacy states of Andhra Pradesh, Bihar, Uttar Pradesh, Madhya Pradesh, and Rajasthan.

The DPEP programme was launched in Orissa in the year 1996-97. Initially eight districts namely Bolangir, Dhenkanal, Gajapati, Kalahandi, Rayagada, Baragarh, Keonjhar and Sambalpur districts were covered under the scheme under World Bank assistance in the 1st phase and was extended to eight more districts such as Koraput, Malknagiri, Nawarangpur, Sonepur, Boudh, Mayurbhanj, Nuapada and Kandhamal with DFID assistance of a project cost of Rs. 313.80 crore in the 2nd phase. By the end of 2003-04 1,578 numbers of new primary schools (734 numbers in DPEP Ph-1 scheme and 844 numbers in DPEP Ph-2 scheme) have been opened in existing DPEP districts with enrolment of 50,697 students (27,472 children in phase 1 and 23,225 children in phase 2 scheme) 5,775 Para teachers were engaged in these schools including 1,978 para teachers in DPEP phase 1 schools. Besides 42-lakh free textbooks have been distributed in DPEP districts among the students and all the students have been provided with this experimental edition.

(C) Mid-day Meal Programme

National Programme for Nutritional Support to Primary Education was started on 15th August, 1995, popularly known as the school meal programme to increase enrolment, retention, and attendance in primary classes by providing supplementary nutrition to all children in primary school. The scheme has spread throughout the country 100 gm of food grains in the form of cooked meal is given to every child per school day in classes 1 to 5. By 1997-98 110 million children in primary classes were covered under this scheme. Evaluate report have confirmed the positive impact on student enrolment and retention.

The Mid-day Meal Scheme was revised and universalized at Primary level with effect from September, 2004 to make a provision for providing cooked meals to children studying in government, government-aided, and local body schools and EGS&AIE centres. Besides providing foodgrains free of cost to the States/UTs, and foodgrains transportation subsidy, the Central Government provides assistance for converting foodgrains into cooked meal at a rate of Re. 1 per child per day. The programme now covers nearly 12 crore children studying in over 9 lakh primary.

Government introduced a Mid-Day Meal Programme from July 1995 throughout the state. During 2003-04, 46.32 lakh children in 51,931 schools were brought under the programme of which cooked meal was provided to 16.39 lakh children and the balance 29.93-lakh children were provided with dry ration. These 46.32 lakh children belong to the schools under school and mass education department as well as NLEP schools, special schools of women and child development department and schools under ST and SC development department.

(D) National Literacy Mission (NLM)

National literacy mission (NLM) was set-up in May 1998 following an objective assessment of the strengths and weaknesses of the earlier programme and to accord a new sense of urgency, seriousness and emphasis with fixed goals, clear timeframe and age specific target groups. Emphasis was laid not on mere enrolment of learners but on attainment of certain predetermined norms and parameters of literacy, innumeracy, functionality, and awareness along with institutionalization of post-literacy and continuing education in a big way.

Achievements of NLM

1. The literacy rate in 2001 has been recorded at 64.8% as against 52.21% in 1991. The 12.59% points increase in the literacy rate during the period is the highest increase in any decade.
2. 118.20 million persons made literate as on 31st March, 2004.
3. Rate of growth in literacy is more in rural areas than in urban areas.
4. The gap in male female literacy rate has decreased from 24.84% in 1991 to 21.60% in 2001.
5. Female literacy increased by 14.41, i.e., from 39.29 to 53.7, whereas male literacy increased by 11.17, i.e., from 64.13 during the last decade.
6. Gender equity and women's empowerment is also visible as about 60% of participants and beneficiaries are women.
7. The population in 7+ age group increased by 171.6 millions while 203.6 million additional persons became literate during 1991-2001.
8. All the states and union territories without expectation have shown increase in literacy rates during 1991-2001.

9. In all states and union territories the male literacy rate is now over 60 per cent Kerala continues to have the highest literacy rate of 90.92 and Bihar has the lowest literacy rate of 47.53.

10. Significant decline in absolute number of non-literates from 328.88 million in 1991 to 304 million in 2001. Out of the total 600 districts in the country, 596 districts have been covered by NLM under literacy programme.

(E) Sarva Siksha Abhiyan (SSA)

A landmark programme of SSA, is the first ever nation wide programme for UEE seeks to reach every child in every hamlet in the country in the prescribed time trend and the Constitution of India was amended in 2002 to make education a fundamental right of every child. It is a flagship programme of the Government of India launched in 2001-2002 in the new millennium. It seeks to achieve the goal of universal primary education by 2005 and the goal of UEE by 2010. This would mean that children in all states would complete at least five years of schooling or its equivalent through the non-formal means by the year 2005. SSA is an effort to universalize elementary education by community ownership of the school system. It is a response to the demand for quality basic education all over the country. It is also an attempt to provide an opportunity for improving human capabilities to all children through provision of community owned quality education in a mission mode.

Meaning of SSA

1. A programme for clear timeframe for universal elementary education.
2. A response to the demand for quality basic education all over the country.
3. An opportunity for promoting social justice through basic education.
4. An effort at effectively involving the Panchayati Raj institutions, school management committees, village and urban slum level education committees, parents-teachers association mother-teacher associations tribal autonomous councils and other grass root level structures in the management of elementary schools.
5. An expression of political will for universal elementary education across the country.
6. A partnership between the Central, State and the local government.
7. An opportunity for states to develop their own vision of elementary education.

Aims of SSA

The SSA seeks to provide useful and relevant elementary education to all children in six to fourteen age groups by 2010. Its other goal is to bridge social, regional, and gender gaps with the active participation of the community in the management of schools. It is a quest for an educational system that does not alienate the child from the society and seeks to promote community solidarity. The children are slowed to learn about their natural environment in a manner that harnesses the human potential, both spiritually and materially. The stress is on value-based learning which gives opportunities to children to work for other's well-being rather than to permit selfish pursuits. SSA realizes the value of early childhood care and education and looks upon the 0-14 age as a continuum. It will try to support pre-school learning in ICDs centres or special pre-school centres in non-ICDs.

Education is indispensable to economic development. Education mainly female education affects the income considerably and plays an important role in controlling fertility, empowers women and accelerates economic growth of the country.

✲✲✲

Chapter 3

HEALTH AND WOMEN

The three essential choices for people in an economy are: (i) to acquire knowledge (ii) to lead a long and healthy life, and (iii) to have access to the resources needed for a descent standard of living. Of course social development does not end here; there are other choices, range from political, economic and social freedom, enjoying self-respect and guarantee of human rights. The 1995 Human Development Report clearly added the gender equity and empowerment dimension to the concept of human development. The HDR observes that:

Human development encompasses' elements that constitute the critical issues of gender and development. There are four major elements in the concept of human development: (1) productivity, (2) equity, (3) sustainability, and (4) empowerment. Through enhanced capabilities, the creativity and productivity of people must be increased so that they become effective agents of growth. Economic growth must be combined with equitable distribution of its benefits and equitable opportunities must be available both to present and to future generations. And all people, women and men, must be empowered to participate in the design and implementation of key decisions that shape their lives. Human development is impossible without gender equality. As long as women are excluded from the development process, development will remain weak and lopsided.

One of the major gender issues is women's health. During pre-independent period maternal and infant mortality rates were the main concern for women's health in India. But after independence the health programmes concentrated on maternal and child health. The pre-natal and post-natal care, attention to hygienic conditions, adequate diet during pregnancy, safe delivery system and information on birth control methods to men and women were taken up to promote healthy womanhood in general and health of women in particular. In spite of all these programmes for the up keep of the health of the women, the health condition of the women has not been improved significantly.

The committee on Status of Women in India (1974) for the first time revealed a great concern about the declining sex ratio since the beginning of the 20th Century. It clearly indicates the declining health status of women in the country. Along with aspects of maternal health, life expectancy, access to health services and nutritional status, etc., have drawn attention to the gender dimensions of women's health.

The forces working at homes, workplaces, society and the state determine women's health. Burden of hardship falls disproportionately on women due to six types of inequality:

(1) Mortality, due to gender bias in health care and nutrition,

(2) Natal destruction that is sex selective abortion and female infanticide,

(3) Lack of basic facility of education and skill development,

(4) Lack of special opportunity for higher education and professional training,

(5) Lack of employment opportunity and promotion in the job, and

(6) Denial of ownership rights to women in acquiring house, land and other property.

Sex Ratio

Sex ratio is fairly a good indicator of female status in society. High sex ratio is synonym of higher status of women. The data of sex ratio of 15 major selected states of India for the period 1901-2001 have been presented in the Table 3.1.

In most of the states like A.P. Bihar, Gujarat, Karnataka, M.P, Maharashtra, Orissa, Rajasthan, TN, UP and WB a decadal growth rate of sex ratio can be observed. A remarkable increase in sex ratio has been noticed in Kerala where the ratio is 1,058 according to 2001 Census, which is the highest among all states. There were four states of Kerala, Bihar, Orissa and Tamil Nadu where the sex ratio was more than 1,000 in the year 1901 but by the end of the century, only Kerala has the ratio more than 1,000 in the rest of the states it exhibited declining trend, of course higher than the national figures. Fig.3.1 shows the trend of the change during the century. Contrary to it, Rajasthan occupied the lowest rank in sex ratio as per 2001 Census where the number of females per thousand males is only 848. So far as Orissa is concerned up to 1961, the sex ratio in Orissa has maintained four digit figures but from 1971 onwards, it has been decreasing continuously. The sex ratio in Orissa was 972 and it occupied 4th position among all states. These figures are enough evident to show the basis of low degree of gender disparity in the states of Kerala and TN and high degree of gender disparity in the states of Bihar and Rajasthan. The ratio has been decreasing continuously for India. In the year 1901, it was 972 and in 2001, the ratio was 933, which indicates clear gender discrimination.

The 2001 Census is a pointer to an alarming position in progressive and developed states like Maharashtra and Punjab have very low-level sex ratio of 922 and 793 respectively. The prosperous states like Maharashtra with its sugar belt and Punjab and Hariyana with their green revolution do not indicate any better treatment to their women folk. Kerala with good educational system, strong public health system and reasonably equitable distribution of wealth resulted in healthy indicators where the sex ratio is as high as 1,058 females per 1,000 men in the state. Surprisingly, the backward communities of tribal people, the sex ratio is higher, there is due respect and rights given to women folk than the so-called higher class people.

Table 3.1

Sex Ratio in India and the States 1901-2001

State	*1901*	*1941*	*1951*	*1961*	*1971*	*1981*	*1991*	*2001*
AP	985	980	986	981	977	975	972	978
Assam	919	875	868	869	896	910	923	932
Bihar	1061	1002	1000	1005	957	948	907	921
Gujarat	954	941	952	940	934	942	934	921
Haryana	861	869	871	868	867	87	865	861
Karnataka	983	960	966	959	957	963	960	964
Kerala	1004	1027	1028	1022	1016	1032	1036	1058
MP	972	946	945	932	920	921	912	920
Maharashtra	978	949	941	936	930	937	934	922
Orissa	1037	1053	1022	1001	988	981	971	972
Punjab	832	836	844	845	865	879	882	874
Rajasthan	905	906	921	908	911	919	910	848
TN	1044	1012	1007	992	978	977	974	986
UP	938	907	998	907	876	882	876	898
WB	945	852	865	878	891	911	917	934
India	972	945	946	941	930	934	937	933

Source: Census Report, 2001, Govt. of India.

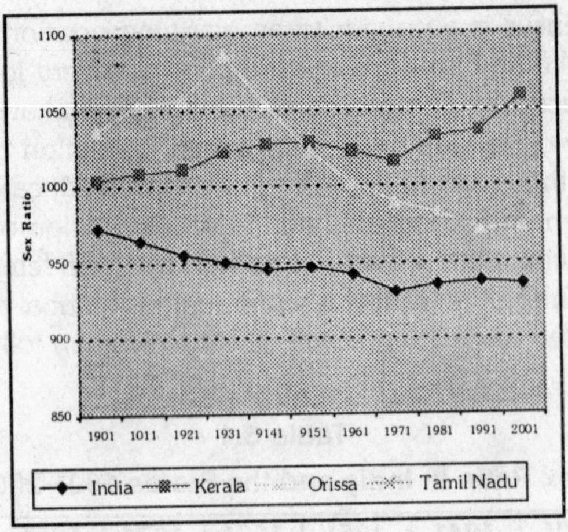

Fig.3.1: Sex Ratio during Twentieth Century: India

The modern technology instead of helping the mothers to preserve their health in one case at least it is regarded as harmful to the women. In the, 80s of last century the sex detection tests started and slowly grown the incidence of sex selective abortions, known as female foeticide. Sex detection clinics are mushrooming even in the rural areas and in spite of some legal restrictions female foeticide are going on rampantly. When the world is trying to raise the status of women we in India use the advanced technology for the elimination of female children.

Table 3.2

Life Expectancy at Birth in Major States of India 2001-2006

	State	*Life expectancy at birth (2001-06)*		
		Male	**Female**	**Gap**
	INDIA	63.87	66.91	3.04
1	Andhra Pradesh	62.79	65.00	2.21
2	Assam	58.96	60.87	1.91
3	**Bihar**	**65.66**	**64.79**	**-0.87**
4	Gujarat	63.12	64.10	0.98
5	Haryana	64.64	69.44	4.66
6	Karnataka	62.43	66.44	4.01
7	Kerala	71.67	75.00	3.33
8	**Madhya Pradesh**	**59.19**	**58.01**	**-1.18**
9	Maharashtra	66.75	69.76	3.01
10	**Orissa**	**60.05**	**59.71**	**-0.34**
11	Punjab	69.78	72.00	2.22
12	Rajasthan	62.17	62.80	0.63
13	Tamil Nadu	67.00	69.75	2.75
14	Uttar Pradesh	63.54	64.09	0.55
15	West Bengal	66.08	69.34	3.26

Source: Ministry of Health and Family Welfare, Govt. of India.

Life Expectancy at Birth (LEB)

The LEB is an important indicator of quality of life. The figures of life expectancy and the gender gap have been shown in Table 3.2. It shows relatively higher life expectancy rates of female over male for the years 2001-2006. The life expectancy of India has increased both for male and female. A remarkable increase has been marked in life expectancy for India for the year 2001-2006, which is 65.93 for total, 63.87 for male and 66.91 for female. Female have greater life expectancy at birth than males in most of the countries of the world. This holds well in case of India also. But it is reverse in case of Orissa, Bihar and Madhya Pradesh, which indicates deep-rooted bias against women from birth. Table 3.3 presents life expectancy at birth in India and Orissa. This table shows that the life expectancy of females always remained higher in India from 1981-86 but females life expectancy remained less than males in Orissa.

Table 3.3

Life Expectancy at Birth in India and Orissa

Year	*India*		*Orissa*		*Gender Gap Orissa*
	Male	*Female*	*Male*	*Female*	
1971-81	50.90	50.00	51.93	49.59	2.34
1981-86	55.60	56.40	54.13	51.90	2.23
1986-91	58.10	59.10	57.13	55.15	1.98
1991-96	60.60	61.70	60.13	58.40	2.09
1996-01	62.80	64.20	62.13	61.15	0.98
2001-06	63.87	66.91	60.05	59.79	0.26

Source: Orissa Budget at a Glance, 2005-2006.

Individual figures of male, female and total life expectancy index (LEI) are calculated for selected states of India during 1998-2002. The figures are shown in Table 3.4. The LEI is highest in Kerala with index of 0.806 and lowest of 0.531 in MP. Nine states are above the national index while six states are below it.

It is by now well-documented that the health status of women in India is extremely low, which is rather ironic as women are the primary caretakers of the household's health. Neglect of women's health stems from cultural practices favouring males. But faulty policy planning too has ensured that women remain the most disadvantaged in terms of health. One such faulty planning refers to the misplaced emphasis on uteri-centricity or reproduction-centred policies. While maternal and reproductive health issues constitute an important area of women's health, they are by no means the only ones that need to be addressed. There is the necessity of examining other equally important health issues such as:

- Gender bias in nutrition
- Higher female mortality
- Inadequate availability of health care and access to medical services.

Table 3.4

Index of Life Expectancy in Major States of India 1998-2002

State	*Total LEI*	*Male LEI*	*Female LEI*
Kerala	0.806	0.763	0.848
Punjab	0.724	0.706	0.741
Maharashtra	0.687	0.667	0.706
TN	0.671	0.653	0.688
Haryana	0.668	0.661	0.673
Karnataka	0.658	0.630	0.686
WB	0.651	0.638	0.663
Gujarat	0.640	0.623	0.656
AP	0.638	0.616	0.660
India	0.624	0.610	0.638
Rajasthan	0.601	0.591	0.610
Bihar	0.591	0.606	0.575
UP	0.566	0.573	0.558
Orissa	0.558	0.556	0.558
Assam	0.548	0.545	0.510
MP	0.531	0.534	0.528

Source: Following the measure of UNDP, the index numbers compiled by the author.

Mortality Ratios

The two mortality ratios namely Maternal Mortality Ratio (MMR) and Infant Mortality Ratio (IMR) are the vital indicators of the status of health of women. The two ratios also control the expectancy of life at birth. The life expectancy at birth was 41 years in the year 1961 which increased to 65 years by the end the century. Maternal mortality ratio is one of the highest in India; it is now 407 per lakh of population. The MMR is about 13 per cent higher in the rural sector.

The causes of high MMR in India can be divided into two: (1) Medical causes, and (2) Social factors. The medical causes again can be divided into two categories: (i) Obstetric causes, and (ii) Non-obstetric causes.

Medical Factors: The important obstetric causes of maternal mortality are: (1) Haemorrhage, (2) Toxaemia or high blood pressure, (3) Anaemia or bloodiessness, (4) Abstracted labour, (5) Perpetual sepsis or infection of the mothers after delivery, and (6) Death as result of unsafe abortions, (7) Mal-position of child in the womb at the time of delivery. The non-obstetric causes include: (1) Anaemia or bloodlessness, (2) the associated diseases of cardiac, renal, hepatic, metabolic, etc., infections, (3) malignancy and accident of the mother during pregnancy.

Social Factors: The social factors are equally responsible for MMR or so to say more responsible for the high rate of MMR in our country. Some of the important factors are: (1) age of mother during the pregnancy, (2) too close pregnancy of the mothers and larger family size, (3) poverty and malnutrition, (4) illiteracy, (5) ignorance and prejudices, (6) non-availability of maternity services nearby, and shortage of healthy man-power, (7) delivery of the child by untrained old ladies of the village instead of trained nurses, and (8) poor environmental condition in the house and in the neighbour hood.

Maximum of about 45 per cent of maternal deaths are caused by two factors of haemorrhage and anaemia. Non-availability of proper food during the pregnancy and unreachable health facilities to the pregnant mothers in the rural sector are the main causes of these two types of death. The percentage of mortality factors according to the rank of the cause is shown in Table 3.5.

Table 3.5

Rank of Causes of Maternal Mortality in India

Rank	*Cause of Death*	*Per cent*
1	Haemorrhage and Puerperium	25.2
2	Anaemia	19.6
3	Abortions	13.7
4	Toxaemia or high blood pressure	12.6
5	Perpetual sepsis	11.5
6	Mal-position of the child	8.5
7	Other causes	8.9
	Total	**100**

Most of the death of the mothers during and immediately after the delivery of the child is due to the fact that even today only 46.9 per cent of the deliveries are made in hospitals and maternity homes under the supervision of doctors and experts. Of course good improvement has been made during the second half of the 20th Century. In mid-20th Century the institutional deliveries remained 33.6 per cent and almost cent per cent deliveries in the rural sector were at the home with the help of older village ladies.

Maternal Mortality Rate (MMR)

The number of maternal deaths per 1,00,000 live births is a significant yardstick to gauge woman's health status. The high mortality rate among women as revealed by maternal deaths due to sepsis, anaemia, toxaemia, haemorrhage, and abortions, indicate that women's health in general, and reproductive health in particular, remain largely neglected. Poor nutrition of girls especially in childhood and adolescent has serious consequences. It is not just early marriages and adolescent child-bearing that leads to this situation, but the low level of health service utilisation and the poor quality of health care received during pregnancy are also responsible for both high levels of neonatal and maternal mortalities. In addition, the burden of work shouldered by women gives rise to constraints making it difficult to seek health care. The reproductive morbidity profiles of women, which include gynaecological, obstetrical and contraceptive morbidity is an area that needs careful examination.

In India, the maternal mortality was not known 100 years back, but Public Health Commission mentioned it was approximately 2000. There is the frantic preference for a male-child in India and in the process about 40 lakh mothers risk their lives and get illegal abortion done. Many pregnant women die in the process most of which neither are reported by their parents nor by those who carry out those sex selective abortions. The World Health Organisation (WHO) in the year 2000 estimated that bout 150 lakh illegitimate abortions take place in the world, most of which are taking place in Asian countries. It states that out of total abortions 67 lakh are done in unhygienic conditions there by risking the women to a host of infections leading to death. A study conducted in metropolitan city of Delhi reveals that about 18 per cent of abortions done are legally justified according to the provisions of Medical Termination of Pregnancy Act.

Over the years, the maternal mortality in India has declined, but in comparison to developed countries, it is very high. While reviewing the available statistics on maternal deaths, there is a wide interstate variation. In the states like Kerala, Maharashtra and Punjab, the MMR is 87,336 and 369 respectively, while in states like Orissa, Madhya Pradesh and Uttar Pradesh, the MMR is 738,711 and 624 respectively. National Family Health Survey, 1992-93 has reported maternal mortality rate of 437 per 1,00,000 live births which only declined to 407 by the year 1998. The rural MMR is 448, 13 per cent higher than the urban MMR. The MMR duing 2004-06 is 254 per 1,00,000 live birth for India, whereas it was recorded 303 for Orissa during the same period.

Infant Mortality Rate (IMR)

Infant mortality rate is a key indicator of the general health status of a population. The IMR which was 122 per 1,000 live births in 1961, reduced to 55 by the year 2008. It was targeted to reduce the IMR to 45 per 1,000 by the end of the Tenth Plan period in 2007 and 28 per 1,000 by the end of 11th Five-Year Plan. As per the report of the Sample Registration System issued by the Registrar General of India, the Infant Mortality Rate of Orissa was 87 per thousand live births in 2002 against the national average of 64. With a view to reducing the same to a level of 60 by 2005, the state government have launched a mission under the caption "Infant Mortality Reduction Mission".

IMR is one of the important factor that influence the life expectancy at birth. Table 3.6 depicts the rate of infant mortality and gender gap in major states of India for the year 1961, 2006, 2007 and 2008.

Table 3.6

State-wise Infant Mortality Rate by Sex & Residence (per 1000 live birth)

Sl. No.	*States/Union Territories*	*1961*			*2006*			*2007*			*2008*		
		Male	*Female*	*Gap*	*Male*	*Female*	*Gap*	*Male*	*Female*	*Gap*	*Male*	*Female*	*Gap*
1	Andhra Pradesh	100	82	-18	55	58	3	54	60	6	51	54	3
2	Assam	N.A.	N.A.	N.A.	67	68	1	66	68	2	62	65	3
3	Bihar	95	94	-1	58	63	5	58	59	1	53	58	5
4	Gujarat	81	84	3	52	54	2	52	60	8	49	51	2
5	Haryana	87	119	32	57	58	3	55	60	5	51	57	6
6	Karnataka	87	74	-13	46	50	4	47	52	5	44	46	2
7	Kerala	55	48	-7	14	16	2	13	14	1	13	12	-1
8	Madhya Pradesh	158	140	-18	72	77	5	72	77	5	68	72	4
9	Maharashtra	96	89	-7	35	36	1	34	41	7	33	33	0
10	Orissa	119	111	-8	73	74	1	71	73	2	68	70	2
11	Punjab	74	79	5	39	50	11	43	47	4	39	43	4
12	Rajastan	114	114	0	65	69	4	75	72	-3	60	65	5
13	Tamil Nadu	89	82	-7	36	37	1	35	38	3	30	33	3
14	Uttar Pradesh	131	128	-4	70	73	3	69	72	3	64	70	6
15	West Bangal	103	57	-46	37	40	3	37	39	2	34	37	4
	All India	**122**	**108**	**-14**	**56**	**59**	**3**	**55**	**61**	**6**	**52**	**55**	**3**

Source: Economic Survey 2004-05, 2005-06, 2007-08; SRS, Vol.44 No. 1 Oct 2009; Office of Registrar General, Ministry of Home Affairs

Infant mortality rate is a key indicator of the general health status of a population:

Table 3.6 shows the male and female IMR and gap between the two in major states of India. The IMR which was 122 for male in 1961 in India was reduced to 52 during the first decade of 21 century (2008). The female IMR was 1961 reduced to 55 from 108 during the same period. In 1961 the male IMR in more than female (-14), but gradually the IMR of female started increasing and the gap was reduced to 3 in the year 2008. It clearly shows that gender discrimination has increased towards the end of the 20th and begining of 21st century. This may be due to:

- Illiteracy on lack of education among the females:
- Gender discrimination removes the initial biological survival advantage of females, resulting in excess female mortality over the age of one.
- Demographic factors such as birth order, maternal age and birth intervals also affects mortality rate significantly.
- Lack of maternal care during pregnancy, including lack of improved nutrition, iron foliate, tetanus, immunisation and treatment of maternal infection etc.
- Lack of awareness among men, who can play important roles in enabling women to deliver in institutions providing transportation and funds and sharing in case of children (World Bank 2008).
- Poverty and other individual on household factors have a profound influence on child nutrition health and survival.

Infant mortality rate in India gradually declining but the IMR of the females is not declining rapidly to catch up the IMR of the males. Male IMR declined from 96 in 1980 to 52 in 2008, but female IMR declined to 55 during the same period. With the exception of 1991, in all other years the IMR of females remained higher to male IMR.

Figures of male and female IMR from the year 1981 to 2002 is shown in Table 3.7.

Table 3.7

The IMR of Males and Females in India

Year	*Male*	*Female*	*Persons*
1980	96	98	97
1991	81	80	80
2000	67	69	68
2002	62	65	64
2008	52	55	53

It is found that in all the South-Eastern including Australia, Japan has IMR of 3 only followed by Australia with 6 and in comparison to world's average IMR at 56. In all the counties with the exception of Pakistan, the female IMR remained higher to the males. The IMR, fertility rate and life expectancy at birth for males and females are presented in Table 3.8.

Table 3.8

The IMR and Life Expectancy Years in East Asian Countries

Country	*Fertility, Rate*	*IMR*	*Expectation of Life*	
			Male	*Female*
China	1.83	37	68.9	78.3
Japan	1.32	3	77.9	85.1
Indonesia	2.35	42	64.8	68.8
Malaysia	2.90	10	70.8	75.5
Bangladesh	3.46	64	61.0	61.8
India	3.01	64	63.2	64.6
Pakistan	5.08	87	61.2	60.9
Sri Lanka	2.01	20	69.9	75.5
Australia	1.70	6	76.4	79.4
Developed Countries	1.56	8	72.1	70.0
Less Developed Countries	2.96	61	61.7	65.1
World	**2.69**	**56**	**63.3**	**67.6**

Source: UNDP, Human Resource Development Report, 2003.

Table 3.9 shows IMR of India and Orissa between 1981 and 2008. It shows that even though the IMR was reduced by 35.56 per cent in 26 years, but in case of Orrisa it is still highest among the states of India.

Table 3.9

Infant Mortality Rate: 1981-2008

Year	*National*	*Orissa State*
1981	110	135
1991	80	124
1995	74	103
1996	72	96
1997	71	96
1998	72	98
1999	70	97
2000	68	96
2001	66	90
2002	64	87
2003	60.0	83
2004	58	77
2005	58	75

2006	57	73
2007	55	72
2008	54	69

Source: *Economic Survey*, Government of Orissa, 2003-04. Economic Survey, Govt. of India, 2008-09.

Infant Mortality Index (IMI)

The figures related to the index of infant mortality for male and female have been constructed for the year 2002 presented in Table 3.10. In five states the index for the female infant mortality is higher than the males and in Orissa the female infant mortality registered highest index in the year 2002.

Table 3.10

Index of Infant Mortality in Major States of India 2002

State	*Total*	*Male*	*Female*
AP	0.943	0.946	0.940
Assam	0.929	0.930	0.929
Bihar	0.939	0.944	0.934
Gujarat	0.944	0.945	0.944
Haryana	0.937	0.946	0.927
Karnataka	0.945	0.944	0.947
Kerala	0.989	0.991	0.988
MP	0.915	0.919	0.912
Maharashtra	0.955	0.952	0.958
Orissa	0.913	0.905	0.921
Punjab	0.949	0.962	0.936
Rajasthan	0.917	0.915	0.920
Tamil Nadu	0.955	0.954	0.957
UP	0.92	0.924	0.916
WB	0.951	0.947	0.955
India	**0.936**	**0.938**	**0.935**

Note: *Following the measure of UNDP, the index number having constructed.*

Source: Economic Survey, 2005-06, Govt. of India.

Child Mortality Rate (CMR)

The death of a child in between 0 to 4 years of age is known as Child mortality. Death of child for every 1,000 children is known as the CMR. In India the CMR was 57.3 in the year 1972 which reduced to 19.5 by the year 2000. In the South Asia region with the exception of Pakistan, India has highest CMR of 93 deaths per 1,000 live births.

Female Foeticide

The life of a female child can be summed up in four words: decimation, discrimination, deprivation and degradation. In the first state of life, from conception to childhood, it is decimation and discrimination; in adolescence, deprivation is added; and finally to fuel the furnace in which she suffers, we add degradation, i.e., through abuse, dowry, deaths and *sati*. Mr. Hingrani, the Supreme Court lawyer advocated abortion of female foetus, which not only amounts to discrimination of female child, but also leads to the lowering of the women's status. India's twin pressures of family planning programmes and dowry, especially the former, have brought female foeticide to shameful proportions. Female foeticide is the modern form of female infanticide prevalent in India. Presently with the growth of science and other modern technology to detect the sex of the child to be born, the female foetus is destroyed in the womb, this just the new avatar of female infanticide of the earlier period. The practice of female infanticide was prevalent in few communities but today it is being adopted in all the communities in India.

Female infanticide has been prevalent in India from ancient times. Not only at the lower level of the society, even the elite sections of the society, such as Rajput rulers and Talukdars killed their female children. This practice was common among Jats, Ahirs, Khatris, Gujjars and Leva Kanbis in North Indian states. The British officials coming mostly from the upper strata of the society shocked to find this inhuman system prevalent in India. The British discovered this practice in 1789 and took immediate steps to suppress this practice. Because of this practice there were no female child in Rajput families for centuries together. Female infants barely a few hours old killed easily adding poison with the mother's milk, water or exposing them to extreme heat or cold. There was shortage of females for marriage in the Rajput families, the established brokers purchased girls of marriageable age and sold to the Rajput families for marriage. The British government passed a law in 1870 banning female infanticide but this system could not be suppressed immediately. In modern time the female infanticide took the form of female foeticide.

Mean Age at Marriage (MAM)

A datasheet prepared by Human Resources Development, Government of India in the year 1991 shows nearly 67 per cent of marriages are taking place under the age of 18. In a traditional culture, a women's health is dependent on some of the social factors like age at marriage, search for son preference thus lingering the period of fertility in her life span. Education is an important determinant of status of women in the society. Literacy rate among women is also responsible for high/low rates of MMR, Infant Mortality (IMR), birth and cases of female foeticide and dowry deaths.

Health Care – Global Comparison

In comparison to other Western countries the health care system in India is very poor. In expectancy of life Australia and Canada have highest age of people of 80.5 years; the infant mortality rate is as low as 3 per thousand live births which indicates high health care provisions in these countries. Physicians and nurses per lakh of population are also far higher in the developed countries in comparison to India. In France and Germany number of physicians per one lakh people is the highest in the world with 337 physicians. Nurses attending to the patients are highest in UK with 1,212 nurses per lakh of people followed by Germany and Sweden with 1,024 each.

The figures of life expectancy, infant mortality, physicians and nurses per lakh population are shown in Table 3.11.

Table 3.11

Health Care Indicators in Selected Countries of the World

2002-03

Country	*Life expectancy year*	*Infant Mortality Rate*	*Physicians per lakh people*	*Nurses per lakh people*
Australia	80.5	5.0	247	971
Canada	80.5	5.0	214	995
France	79.5	4.0	337	972
Germany	80.0	4.0	337	1024
Japan	82.5	3.0	198	779
Sweden	80.5	3.0	328	1024
UK	79.5	5.0	230	1212
USA	77.5	6.0	256	937

Source: UNDP, Human Resource Development Report, 2003.

Health Care in India

Availability of health care facilities in India for the people is very poor. Number of hospitals and health centres, doctors, nursing people and beds available are the indicators of health care.

The comparative picture of these indicators between the years 1981 and 2003 is shown in Table 3.12.

Table 3.12

Indicators of Health, 1981-2003

Indicator	*1981*		*2003*	
	No. lakh	*Per lakh people*	*No. lakh*	*Per lakh people*
SC/PHC/CHC	0.58	8	1.64	16
Dispensaries and Hospitals	0.24	3	0.38	4
Beds (Private and Public)	5.70	83	9.15	89
Nursing personnel	1.44	21	8.30	81
Doctors (Modern System)	2.69	39	6.56	64

Source: Economic Survey – 2003-04, Government of India.

Free and well-designed state health services, which are more accessible and affordable to the poorest of the rural poor is also a determining factor for women's health. Anaemia is widely prevalent among women and even rampant in adolescent girls. In India, 60 per cent of women are undernourished with weight less tan 40 kg., 12-30 per cent are stunted and 60 per cent are anaemic by their last trimester of pregnancy. Anaemic women are immune suppressed and experience higher rates of morbidity, especially from urinary and reproductive tract infections, which are associated with Low Birth Weight (LBW) babies, prematurity and growth retardation. Low levels of health service utilisation and the poor quality of health care, overburden of work shouldered by women gives rise to constraints making it difficult for them to seek health care.

Nutritional Needs

In early adolescence, because of a growth spurt associated with puberty and onset of menstruation, nutritional needs of a girl increases, especially of iron, vitamin A, calcium and iodine. Denial of adequate food to girls, partly due to non-availability and partly due to discrimination, continues to be a major problem. An inadequate diet has lifelong consequence for girls, as their growth and development is jeopardised. Early marriage and early pregnancy further deplete their inadequate reserve. Rising food prices, limitations of the public distribution system and shift to non-edible cash crops, has also worsened the existing nutritional status of women. Malnutrition is common among all sections of the Indian population, but is of greatest consequence and seriousness in women. Poor nutritional status and iron deficiency also increase the risks of death and disability especially during pregnancy and childbirth.

Maternal Health

Women throughout her life span experiences number of health problems but much attention is not paid by family, service holder or by women themselves. Not much data is available on general morbidity amongst women. Due to socialisation women in our country have developed a culture of silence. It is hammered into their psyche that being women you have to tolerate everything. Thus, women have developed tremendous capacity of tolerance. The maternal mortality is a tip of iceberg of Indian women's health status. Maternal mortality issue, which has tremendous influence of socio-economic and health condition of our country, including high mortality, high infant and child-mortality, illiteracy, etc. Analysing the situation shows that all the problems are rooted in the lower status of women. Poor health status not only leads to high mortality, but their lower status denies them from opportunities for growth and development including access to food, education, health services. Marriage of women at early age and childbearing at early age results in many health hazards.

The level of maternal mortality is a sensitive index of the prevailing health condition and general socio-economic development of a community. According to the international classification of disease, maternal death is: "The death of a woman while pregnant or within 42 days of termination of pregnancy, irrespective of the duration and the site of the pregnancy from any cause related to or aggravated by the pregnancy or its management, but not from accidental or incidental causes" (WHO, 1977). In most developing countries, women of reproductive age (15-49 years) constitute a little more than one-fifth of the total population. These women are exposed repeatedly to the risk of pregnancy and child bearing and under existing socio-economic conditions due to lack of medical and health facilities are at risk of mortality and morbidity. The death of mother affects the well-being of the children and her family.

Maternal Care Initiatives

(i) Antenatal Care: Antenatal Care (ANC) refers to pregnancy-related health care provided by a doctor or a health worker in a medical facility or at home. The safe motherhood initiative proclaims that all pregnant women must receive basic but professional ANC. ANC can contribute significantly to the reduction of maternal morbidity and mortality because it also includes advice on the correct diet and provision of folic acid tablets to pregnant women, besides medical care. Despite a vast health care infrastructure, lack of antenatal care is the prime reason behind maternal mortality. Improved nutritional status, coupled with improved ANC, can help to reduce the incidence of low birth weight babies and thus reduce parental, neonatal and infant mortality.

According to the NFHS, 1992, for 27 per cent of the births, antenatal care was provided by allopathic doctors, and for 9 per cent of births antenatal care was given outside the home by other health professionals, such as auxiliary nurse-midwives, lady health visitors, ayurvedic and homoeopathic doctors. For 16 per cent of births, the mothers received antenatal care at home from a health worker. Mothers who had not sought antenatal care outside the home gave reasons of lack of knowledge of services, lack of realisation of safe motherhood, financial cost and lack of time. As expected, antenatal care is more common in urban areas 7.5 per cent than in rural areas of 47 per cent.

(ii) Vaccination: Another major indicator of maternal care is the Tetanus Taxied Vaccine (TTV). The TTV is an important cause of death among neonatal in

India. Neonatal tetanus is a particular problem in Orissa, Madhya Pradesh and Uttar Pradesh, where the proportion of all deaths due to neonatal tetanus is higher than the state's share in the total population of India. Neonatal tetanus is caused by infection of the new born (usually at the time of umbilical stump) with tetanus organism. Neonatal tetanus is most common when the delivery takes place in an unhygienic environment and non-sterilised instruments are used for cutting the umbilical cord. Tetanus typically develops during the first or second week of life and is fatal in 70 to 90 per cent of cases. Where this disease is most common, such as in rural areas of several states, expert medical health is also rarely available thereby leading to a particularly high fatality rate. However, neonatal tetanus is preventable disease. Two doses of TTV given to the pregnant women one month apart during early pregnancy are nearly 100 per cent effective in preventing tetanus in newborns and among mothers.

(iii) Iron and Folic Acid Tablets: Iron and Folic Acid tablets are also one of the major constraints of maternal care programme. The size of woman's baby, her preparation for lactation, and the child depends upon the mother's nutritional status at the time of conception as well as her diet during pregnancy. More maternal care is important for the healthy intrauterine growth of the baby and may affect the baby's birth weight. The provision of iron and folic acid tablets as a prophylaxis against nutritional anaemia among pregnant woman forms an integral part of the MCH activities of the Indian family welfare programme. It is recommended that a pregnant woman should take 100 tablets of iron and folic acid during her pregnancy, and this intake mostly falls short in case of Indian women.

(iv) Place of Delivery: From the standpoint of child survival and health of the mother, the first priority for delivery care is that it is safe and clean. The majority of maternal deaths and much of the chronic morbidity resulting from childbirth are due to the failure to get timely help for complications at delivery. It is essential that delivery be conducted under proper hygienic conditions with the assistance of trained medical practitioners. However, only one-quarter of deliveries in India take place in medical institutions and two-thirds are unattended by a trained medical professional, and a large majority of deliveries are likely to take place without proper hygienic care and timely professional help when complications develop. The situation is particularly serious in rural areas where five out of every six births take place at home and medical assistance is not available for three quarters of births.

(v) Family Planning: Even though India was the first country in the world to take up family planning as an official programme in 1952, achievements over the past 50-plus years have not been as good as would be desirable. There is great need for family planning, both among an increasing number of men who wish to exercise responsibility, their right to parenthood. Nearly all developing countries have family planning programmes, but the degree of political and economic support and their effective reach, vary widely.

Delaying the first and spacing subsequent births are important for the health of women and children, apart from their effects on population growth. Maternal and child health care services, of which family planning programmes are an integral part, should be given the same priority in health services as other elements of primary health care.

Empowering Women for Health

Health is an aspect of women's lives over which they have little or no control. Movements for empowering women to take charge of their health have started in several parts of our country by various organisations. Two key features of this approach are described below:

Self-help: This stems from the realisation that women have been dispossessed of knowledge about their own bodies, by both society and the medical profession. The goal of self-help is to put information and control in the hands of women, developing a health care system that meets their needs. Teaching women about the manner in which their bodies function, and the use of home and herbal remedies are the two cornerstones of this approach. This not only allows women to understand the body and its problems better, they are also more likely to obtain appropriate health care earlier and on their own terms.

Advocacy for Health: Knowledge about the body and herbal remedies for simple complaints are a major step towards women gaining control over their own health, but not the final step in this direction. Women will continue to need the public health care system to meet other health needs. Unfortunately, this system, even at its best, is unable to deliver many of the services required by women. Keeping this reality in mind, women in many parts of the country have organised themselves into groups and are demanding better treatment and services from the public system.

Mental Health

Women's health not only confined to the deteriorated physical health but also the mental trauma that discriminate between the sexes within the family and in the society. The constitution of the body of women is such that it continuously changes its physical form and gives mental stress in different forms. The physical changes of women's body during puberty, the starting of menstruation and the resulting hormonal changes cause psycho-somatic disorders, and mental stress in almost all adolescent girls. Similarly, women face irritation, mood swings and depression caused by the hormonal changes during menopause.

The main types of stressful situation arise during lifetime of a woman requires special health care to tackle different types of stress faced by woman. The tresses can be divided into the following ones:

Economic Stress

- Inadequate food for the family. In most of the poor families even in the middle-class families the women folk take food after the food taken by the male members of the family, whatever remains for eating.

- When there is inadequate financial situation in the family even then the male members first enjoy them whether health care, clothing or in other facilities in the house; women get neglected.
- The financial resources are not handedover to the women folk and the ownership of land or other properties are not rested with women.

Social Stress:

- Women are given low status in the family and in the society. In every family birth of a son is welcomed while birth of a girl is bad luck. They treat them as if they are domestic animals; no preference of their own and no rights in the family matters.
- The *pardha* system in the Hindu families and *burkha* in Muslim community restrict the women's right to go outside the home for different type of work. Of course in the lower strata of the society this is comparatively less.
- The most important stress is dowry system prevailed at the time of marriage. Demand of abnormal dowry makes the women help less at the time of marriage. And with the required dowry demanded by the groom's family if not fulfilled ultimately the women are tortured leading to murder or suicide of the bride.

Rights Based Approach to Women's Health

In the nineties there was a change in development approach — from meeting identified *needs* to a '*rights* based approach'. This was drawn from the UN Declaration of Universal Human Rights and the International Covenant of Economic, Social and Cultural Rights. The 'Right to Health' approach was reinforced by the many national and global movements to reclaim a woman's right to choose what was best for herself and her health. Struggles around abortion rights are one example. The Rights Based Approach was also founded on the mandated accountability of state health systems to protect and promote women's health. Stronger definitions and claims to entitlements in the realm of women's health were provided by treaties upholding women's rights such as the Convention on the Elimination of All Forms of Discrimination Against Women (CEDAW) and the historical consensus on reproductive rights at the International Conference on Population and Development (ICPD).

While the exact characteristics of the 'rights based approach' are still being examined and definitions are being debated, the UN Commission on Human Rights defines it as "an integration of the norms and standards contained in the wealth of international treaties and declarations into the plans, policies and processes of development". In concrete terms this would mean that the objective of a health intervention would be defined in terms of particular 'rights' – as legally enforceable entitlements. An example is "the right to attainment of the highest standard of reproductive health", drawing from the ICPD. Additionally, when we use rights based approaches, there has to be a high level of accountability in terms of a clear focus on who is responsible for protecting, promoting and providing the right.

In struggles across the globe to assert and claim rights, women have constantly redefined what a given right stands for, and sought to ensure legislation to safeguard the extended definition. For example, the human right to life has been extended to include the right of women who choose to be mothers to "go safely through pregnancy and childbirth" with an assurance of survival. In some contexts it has been used to substantiate the right of women to be free of life-threatening gender based violence. Depending on local realities, international standards could be translated into more specific or related but distinct national laws and policies.

At the national level, adequate laws, policies, institutions, administrative procedures and mechanisms of accountability have to be strengthened. This is essential so that if a woman suffers denial and violations of her right to health, she can easily access redress or complaints mechanisms. Moreover, marginal or vulnerable groups should have a high degree of access to information and meaningful participation in development processes and institutions. This would also mean that minority or indigenous women, rural women or women with special needs would be able to have a voice in designing and monitoring policies and programmes for their health needs.

Training for Women's Health

One of the main challenges in implementing a women's health programme which takes into account their needs, vulnerabilities and social realities, is to develop a strategy to train and reorient different members of the team who will take up this work. It includes training managers, field workers and the community. While most formal experiences are through strictly hierarchical models where teachers exercise all the knowledge and power in relation to the learners, here the facilitators' role is very different. The field workers, manager and the nurse have to slowly build the confidence of women to learn to accept their bodies and start a process of questioning many of their previously held notions. Thus, these workers also need to go through training that will help them to develop sensitivity and empathy towards the women's situation. Even for technically trained persons like doctors, it may involve developing new skills in communicating with women. Experiments have already started in developing training modules for middle level managers, field workers, doctors and nurses to equip them to deliver more sensitive and need-based services to women.

A number of community-based studies are bringing to light the extent of women's health problems. Indian women often tolerate ill-health without complaint.

(a) In a study in rural Maharashtra, researchers found that one in two women interviewed reported an illness in the previous month. They spoke of chronic, non-infectious, longstanding problems, related to their reproductive health, to various aches and pains, or to mental health. Illnesses were often linked to their working and living environment, childbearing and contraception. Almost half tolerated their illnesses without treatment — either they couldn't afford the treatment, or they felt it couldn't be treated, or health facilities were inaccessible.

(b) A considerable proportion of women suffer silently from a range of gynaecological problems — reproductive tract infections (RTIs), menstrual problems, cervical erosion, infertility, uterine prolapsed, and so on. The most frequent complaint is of vaginal discharge. RTIs are acquired through sexual transmission, medical procedures such as IUDs, tubectomy, abortion and childbirth, or from overgrowth of the body's own bacteria. Numerous studies have demonstrated that gynaecological morbidity is a serious problem in India.

(c) 1,00,000 Indian women die of pregnancy-related causes each year. The maternal mortality ratio (number of deaths for every 1,00,000 live births) is 50 times higher than developed countries and six times higher than neighbouring Sri Lanka. The six major causes — hemorrhage, anemia, eclampsia (pregnancy-related hypertension), infection, abortion and obstructed labour — account for 85 per cent of pregnancy-related deaths. There are also a number of background factors: nutrition and health status, age, number of children, marital status, gender disparities, lack of information, socio-economic conditions and poor access to health services all influence maternal mortality and morbidity.

(d) Abortion, which has been legal in India since 1971, accounts for at least 12 per cent of maternal deaths. Only ten per cent of the estimated five million abortions (MTP) that take place in India annually are performed in approved health services.

- Authorized MTP centres are concentrated in the urban areas, and in a few states. Many approved centres may not be providing services, many are inadequately equipped, with poorly-trained or insufficient staff. The private sector provides a large proportion of services.
- A rural community-based study in the state of Maharashtra found that one out of six women who underwent an abortion did so to abort a female foetus. Two out of three suffer health consequences serious enough to affect their daily lives. Less than one-third of women are counselled about the procedure's risks, but more than half are given contraceptive advice, and many are forced to accept contraception in order to get an abortion.

However, women's health problems extend beyond their reproductive health. While maternal mortality and morbidity have been the focus of women's health efforts, public health specialists have argued that mortality data from the government's model registration scheme indicate that communicable diseases are the most significant cause of death for women.

(e) More than one-third of all deaths take place in children under the age of five. In 1999, 98 of every 1,000 children died from an infectious disease before their fifth birthday, placing India 49th out of 187 countries in the under-five mortality rate.

- As many as 4,29,000 children died of diphtheria, peruses (whooping cough), tetanus, measles or polio, in 1998. One in two polio deaths in the world occurs in India. All of these are preventable.
- 7,33,000 children under the age of five died of diarrhoea diseases. (250 million cases annually).
- 7,77,000 children under the age of five died of respiratory infections. (nearly 500 million cases annually).
- 3,33,000 children died of complications following low birth weights. These deaths are preventable through adequate nutrition to mother and child, clean water supply and sanitation, effective immunisation and an accessible health service to provide prompt treatment.

The SAARC Decade of the Girl-Child, 1991-2000

The government of India formulated and announced National Plan of Action for the SAARC decade of girl-child in 1992 as approved by the SAARC forum. The specific goals have been spelt out by the SAARC forum to achieve the following goals:

- Survival and protection of the girl-child and safe motherhood.
- The girl children will have equal status with the boys.
- Special protection would be provided to the girl children belongs to economically and socially deprived and disabled children.

Reproductive and Child Health (RCH)

Reproductive and child health program was launched in 1997 as an integrated programme for the facilities provided to children, mothers and in a view to stabilize population through introducing different methods of family planning measures to improve the quality of life of the women in the society. Women and children constitute 76.7 per cent of the total population of India; hence women are to empower both economically and socially to become equal partners in the development of the nation along with men.

Several schemes have been launched to achieve this goal under the RCH programme; the major programmes *inter alias* are:

1. **Indira Mahila Yojana (IMY):** This scheme was launched in the year 1995-96 first in 200 blocks and later extended to all the blocks in the country. Later on the recommendations of a study team the Mahila Smbridhi Yojana started earlier was merged I the IMY.
2. **Balika Sambridhi Yojana (BSY):** This scheme launched in 1997 with a specific aim to change the community's attitude towards the girl-child; it further recast in the year 1999. Previously a grant of Rs.500 was given to every mother who gave birth to a girl-child for a family below poverty line; according to the new provision in addition to it a

grant Rs. 500 per child is deposited in an interest bearing account in the name of new born girl-child. In addition to it benefit of a scholarship for study is deposited on government approved courses in the same account.

3. ***Rural Women's Development and Empowerment Project (RWPEP):*** This Centrally sponsored project was started in 1998 with an aim of creating an environment for the empowerment of women, start with in six states of Bihar, Haryana, Karnataka, Gujarat, Madhya Pradesh and Uttar Pradesh, to extend it to all other states of India in due course.

4. ***Integrated Child Development Scheme (ICDS):*** The Government of India in order to improve the nutritional status of the girl-child and her mother, and multiple objective of controlling family, reduce infant mortality and maternal mortality started a massive programme called the ICDS in the year 1975. It is a holistic programme of child survival and child development and giving learning opportunities to pre-school children and their mothers.

The main characteristics of the ICDS are:

1. All essential services are provided to child and mother at the village level.
2. Special care is taken for the disadvantaged children.
3. It covers children of 0-6 age group.
4. It takes special care for the pregnant and nursing mothers belongs to socially backward communities.
5. It also covers for the support services like water supply and sanitation.
6. It helps also adolescent girls (11-18 years) into a better future mothers who can also act as an agent of social change.

Presently, the ICDS programme covers the all 4,200 blocks and major urban slums in the country benefiting 2.58 crore children under six years of age. The World Bank provides credit for the ICDS projects for the additional components like construction of buildings for office of the ICDS and godowns.

5. ***National Rural Health Mission (NRHM):*** In April 2005, India launched a National Rural Health Mission (NRHM) to provide health care more effectively to rural people throughout the country, especially in those states with poor public health indicators and inadequate health infrastructure.

- To reduce child and maternal mortality
- Prevent and control communicable and non-communicable diseases
- To stabilize the population

The second phase of Reproductive and Child Health Programme was launched at the same time and subsumed into NRHN. It aimed to reduce the IMR, under five mortality rates, MMR and TFR.

The NRHM aims to "Undertake architectural correction" of the health system to improve public health management and service delivery. And important intervention under NRHM is the 'Janani Suraksha Yoana' which aims to promote institutional deliver and there by reduce maternal and neonatal mortality.

One of the corner stone of the programme is promotion of local health traditions including Ayurveda, Yoga, Unani, Siddha and Homopathy (AYUSH). The NRHM aims to maintain these systems into public health care.

The NRHM plans to increase public spending on health to 2 to 3 percent of GDP, including community financing and risk pooling as a result health care is expected to become more affordable to poor.

Health Budget

Spending on health care in a country as proportion of GDP indicates the health of a nation. In India 1.2 per cent of GDP is being spent on health and medical care programmes. This is far from satisfactory. Neighbouring China spends 2.1 per cent of GDP and a small country Nicaragua spends a high percentage of 6.7 per cent of its GDP on health care programmes. Safe drinking water, sanitation and hygiene are three important aspects of health are neglected in the country which requires development to improve the health condition of the people.

Chapter 4
EMPLOYMENT FOR WOMEN

Women's work and their contribution to the socio-economic development of an economy is crucial. The definition of "work" in the usual sense of the term cannot be applicable to women's work participation. Economists analysing in the strict economic terms believe that women's work is in the private sphere, hence, their work cannot be accepted as a contribution to the national economy for the simple reason that they are not paid for their household work in terms of wage labour. Even the Census data does not enumerate women's work participation in the household work accepting their work as unpaid work.

The statistical invisibility of women's work is a reality, mirroring the deep-rooted social bias against women. Women's contribution to the economy remains 'hidden' because their work, especially in agriculture and the unorganised area, remains unremunerated. This happens basically because there are two types of work: work for which payment is made and work for which payment is not made. The former is regarded as 'productive', and such activities are usually done by men, consequently there is not much variation in the percentage of male workers. But women usually do unpaid work, engaged in activities inside and outside homes and in agriculture for which payment is not made, consequently pushing their work outside the area of definition of 'work'.

Men and women both work, the main issue is the types of work they do, where it is done, how it is done and what rewards/remuneration are obtained. When work is defined in terms of activities performed for pay or profit, there are many activities that remain outside the domain of "work". Consequently, to a great extent women's work remains uncounted and unreflected in the Census. This lacuna has an adverse effect on government policies, status of women, and the perspective of people.

There are in fact seven categories of work performed by women in rural and urban India. These are:

(i) Wage and salaried employment;

(ii) Self-employment outside the household for profit;

(iii) Self-employment in cultivation and household industry for profit;

(iv) Self-employment in cultivation for own consumption;

(v) Other subsistence activities in allied sectors such as dairying, livestock rearing and fishing, hunting and cultivation of fruit and vegetable gardens;

(vi) Activities related to domestic work, such as fetching fuel, fodder, water, forest produce, repair of dwellings, making cowdung cakes, food preservation, etc., and

(vii) Domestic work such as cooking, cleaning, care of children, the aged and the sick.

The main reasons for the invisibility of women's work from statistical data are:

1. Cultural constructions of women's work,
2. Difficulties in measuring women's work performed in the family,
3. Difficulties in measuring work in agricultural activities and in other unorganised sectors such as in-house construction industry,
4. Women's socialisation in counting their work as insignificant,
5. The dominant social bias to regard men as a head of the family and push home-related, home-based activities to secondary category,
6. Inadequate format of questions, and
7. Intensively of the investigators, especially when the investigators happens to male investigators.

Work of women can be broadly divided into three: (1) Organised sector, (2) Unorganised sector where it is coming under wage employment, the former with regular and fixed payment while in the latter sector there is no fixed wages or fixed days of work for the women, (3) The third sector where the women work but neither they get any fixed remuneration or their work is recognised as productive work or their contribution to the economy. The unorganised work again can be divided into two as: (1) self-employment, and (2) wage employment. In the self-employment which is pursued by the women in the household or outside house there is no fixed wage earnings but earning net profit contribute income to the household income and directly participate in economic activity.(Fig. 4.1)

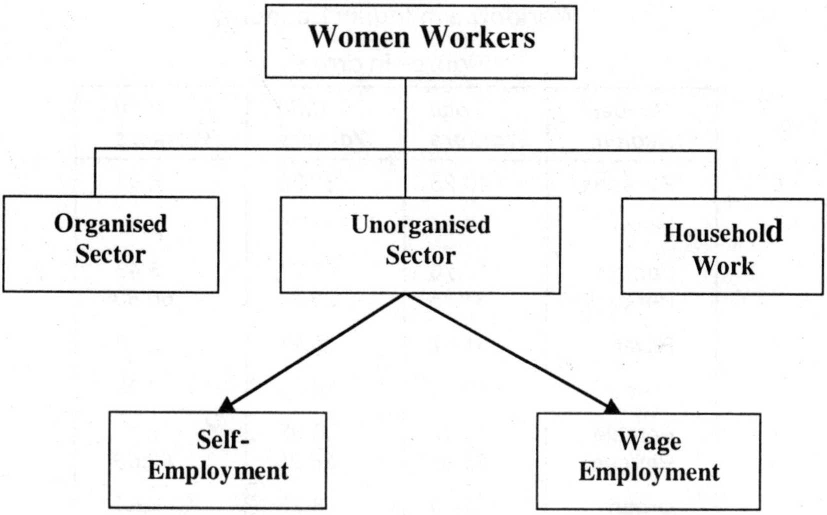

Fig. 4.1 Types of Women Workers

Women in Unorganised Sector

According to 2001 Census, there are 40.25 crore workers in India of all categories which forms 39.26 per cent of total population. Of this, the female workers form 31.55 per cent. The main workers which are 31.32 crore there are 7.27 crore are female workers, which constitutes 23.21 per cent. The main workers are usually accepted in the category of organised sector and marginal workers in the unorganised sector. The marginal workers form 22.19 per cent of the total workforce in the country. The female workers in the marginal workforce constitute 60.80 per cent in the rural sector while in the urban sector their percentage is less than the male workers with 39.28 per cent.

The total workforce and its bifurcation into main and marginal workers with male-female composition is presented in Table 4.1.

Table 4.1

Workforce in Indian Economy

(Figures in crore)

Gender/ Region	*Total Workers*	*Main Workers*	*Marginal Workers*
Persons	40.25	31.32	8.93
Male	27.54	24.05	3.49
Female	12.70	7.27	5.43
Per cent →	*31.55*	*23.21*	*60.80*
Rural	31.07	22.97	8.10
Male	19.92	16.93	2.99
Female	11.14	6.03	5.11
Per cent →	*35.85*	*26.25*	*63.08*
Urban	9.19	8.35	0.84
Male	7.63	7.12	0.51
Female	1.56	1.23	0.33
Per cent →	*16.97*	*14.73*	*39.28*

Source: Census of India 2001.

There is very thin line between the organised and unorganised sectors. The female workers are often pushed from the organised to the unorganised sector and oscillate between skilled and unskilled work according to the demand for work in the market. At the advent of British rule their various economic policies affected handicrafts and artisan industries adversely. Both men and women lost their employment, due to mechanisation. The development of science and technology in the work process displaced self-employed women workers from their traditional occupation.

Displaced Women Workers:

1. When new machines are introduced it displaced manual work. The introduction of rice mills had a devastating impact on women, where as rice husking was a major source of livelihood for women in rural sector.

2. With the coming up of shoe companies the traditional cobblers lost their work. Similarly, the product of potters replaced by plastic industries.

3. Destruction of forest by timber industry lakh of village women lost their livelihood which deprived them of gathering minor forest products.

Non-workers

Women who are not participating in wage/salary employment are shown in the Census data as non-workers. Women folk whatever household work done at home is not included as productive work. Of the 62.27 crore non-workers 59.04 per cent are female. The non-workers can be divided into four categories:

1. Children who are pursuing education or who are not attained the age to participate in the workforce.
2. The senior citizens and older people who are beyond the active work participation age.
3. Those who are unable to work due to ill-health, handicapped or other causes.
4. House wives either skilled or unskilled are not participate in the work-force to earn wages and salaries.

The women in the fourth categories doing household work are majority in the non-working category. They are so to say disguised unemployment. Instead of doing housework if they would have worked outside the house according to their qualification they might have earned good income to supplement the household income. But there is no information about their number and qualification to estimate their income.

The Tenth Five-Year Plan, 2002-2007 has made a major commitment towards empowering women as the agent of socio-economic change and development. The plan suggested a three-fold strategy for empowering women through social, economic and gender justice. Women are generally viewed as the burdens of the society. The contributions towards their families are overlooked. To know the contribution of women the work participation rate is considered as the suitable measure of economic role.

In the present context of the market determining the value of both the commodity and the person, women lose out not because they are not working, but because their work cannot be enumerated and counted in monetary terms. As pointed out by the Shramshakti Report, there are a host of conceptual and methodological problems involved in measuring the economic contribution of women. The data in this sphere is inadequate and grossly underestimates their contribution to family income.

Poor women are mainly engaged as self-employed workers largely in home-based activities, where they work at home intermixes with their household duties and the productivity of their work as well as their status as worker is invisible. Women are undoubtedly engaged in several activities which add to household incomes, but are totally outside the sphere of the market economy. There are numerous activities such as free collection of fodder and fuel, maintaining dairy, poultry and animals, vegetable growing, food processing, sewing, weaving in which women are engaged to increase the "household's command over the necessities". The household would have to spend a lot of money in procuring these services if they were not rendered by women.

Work Participation

The male-female work participation distributed between rural and urban population for the period from 1981 to 2001 Census in India is presented in Table 4.2. During the last two decades of last century the work participation of women workers increased from 23.1 per cent in 1981 to 26.5 in 2001 in the rural sector of the country. There has been no significant increase in the work participation of the women in the urban sector.

Table 4.2

Male-Female Work Participation

(Figures in per cent)

Census		*Female*	*Male*	*Total*
1981	Total	19.7	52.6	36.7
	Rural	23.1	53.8	38.8
	Urban	08.3	49.1	30.0
1991	Total	22.3	51.6	37.5
	Rural	26.5	52.5	40.1
	Urban	09.2	48.9	30.2
2001	Total	25.7	51.9	39.3
	Rural	31.0	52.4	42.0
	Urban	11.6	50.9	32.2

Source: Census of India, Government of India.

Gender-gap in Rural Workforce

In the states the highest work participation of women in 1972-73 was 52.93 per cent in Rajasthan and lowest of 12.8 per cent in West Bengal. By 1999-2000 the position of West Bengal remained same with lowest work participation of women with 16.02 per cent, of course there has been slight improvement in percentage terms from that of 1972-73. At the end of the 20th Century Andhra Pradesh topped in the work participation of women in the rural sector with highest of 47.81 per cent. The gap in the work participation of male and female workers was highest of 37.60 per cent in West Bengal which almost remained same for about two decades as the table shows. The lowest gap of 9 per cent also remained same during the years under study.(Table 4.3)

Table 4.3

Rural Workforce Participation Rate

(Figures in per cent)

State	*1972-73*			*1999-2000*		
	Male	*Female*	*Gap*	*Male*	*Female*	*Gap*
Andhra Pradesh	62.38	45.11	17.27	60.49	47.81	12.68
Bihar	51.60	19.60	32.00	49.19	17.29	31.90
Gujarat	52.30	37.76	14.54	58.43	41.28	17.15
Haryana	49.24	34.22	15.02	47.47	20.20	27.27
Karnataka	57.53	42.97	14.56	59.51	37.98	21.53
Kerala	46.83	25.40	21.43	55.27	23.77	31.51
Madhya Pradesh	56.29	44.02	12.27	53.60	38.19	15.41
Maharashtra	54.61	45.52	9.09	53.11	43.39	9.72
Orissa	57.72	30.73	26.99	55.09	29.88	25.51
Punjab	54.75	26.63	28.12	53.00	28.02	24.98
Rajasthan	57.99	52.93	5.06	49.98	38.80	11.18
Tamil Nadu	60.27	44.42	15.85	59.42	43.03	11.18
Uttar Pradesh	53.29	23.79	29.50	48.10	20.11	27.99
West Bengal	50.48	12.88	37.60	53.39	16.02	37.37

Source: National Accounts Statistics of India, 1950-51 to 2001-02, EPWRF, Mumbai.

Gender-gap in Farm and Non-farm Sector

The rural sector can be divided into: (1) Farm, and (2) Non-farm sectors. In the farm sector most of the states the gender disparity rates declined over the year from 1972-73 to 1999-2000. But in Karnataka, Madhya Pradesh, and Maharashtra, the disparity rate increased over the years. The general work participation in the non-farm sector is low in comparison to the farm sector. The gender disparity ratio is very low in all the states and over the years it further increased with the exception of Maharashtra. In that state the gender gap reduced to 0.58, on the other hand in Kerala, the highest literary state for both male and female the gender gap remained highest of 22.09 per cent in 1999-2000.

Table 4.4

Gender-gap in Farm and Non-farm Sector

State	Farm Sector		Non-farm Sector	
	72-73	99-00	72-73	99-00
Andhra Pradesh	10.23	4.69	7.03	7.99
Bihar	25.84	24.05	6.16	7.89
Gujarat	9.84	3.72	4.71	13.48
Haryana	11.11	9.66	3.90	17.35
Karnataka	10.35	13.40	4.21	8.25
Kerala	11.03	9.50	10.39	22.09
Madhya Pradesh	8.83	10.15	3.44	5.19
Maharashtra	2.98	9.15	6.11	0.58
Orissa	19.54	18.36	3.59	6.19
Punjab	25.81	8.32	2.33	16.65
Rajasthan	0.66	-2.03	4.40	13.21
Tamil Nadu	8.04	4.30	7.80	12.04
Uttar Pradesh	23.06	16.93	6.44	11.07
West Bengal	32.03	26.81	5.56	10.53

Source: National Accounts Statistics of India, 1950-51 to 2001-02, EPWRF, Mumbai.

Women in Organised Sector

The organised sector includes public sector establishments encompassing government services at the Central, state and local levels; public sector undertakings in areas such as agriculture, industry, credit, financing, public utilities/services; and all non-agricultural private establishments which employ 10 or more persons. The participation of women in the organised sector in public and private sector undertakings for the period from 1971 to 2000 is presented in Table 4.5.

The table shows a steady increase in the work participation rate of women in both public as well as private sector. On the other hand the percentage participation of male workforce are in the declining trend in both public and private sectors. The women are more employed in the private sector than in public sector. It causes an increase in the earning of the family, which enables the children to get better education and training. With the advent of a high-mechanised era and automation in all fields, children need to be trained and educated to develop into skilled manpower. Since the number of jobs available in the market is decreasing, trained/skilled manpower is necessary to take up self-employment.

Highly educated women are concentrated in banking, IT, advertising, research and travel. These employ 20-35 per cent women of which 10.20 per cent are at the senior level. A study of 35 corporate houses done by Cerebus Consulting in 2002 found that 15-20 per cent female managers leave after getting married. On the rest 80-90 per cent exit after they have their kids, despite 36 per cent of the companies providing teleworking option, wherein the younger mother could work from home. On the other hand they are successful in the career, due to the family support or from her maid.

Table 4.5

Employment of Women in the Organised Sector

(Figures in lakh)

Year	*Public Sector*	*Private Sector*	*Total*
1971	8.60 (8.0)	10.80 (16.0)	19.40 (11.0)
1981	14.90 (9.7)	12.90 (17.5)	27.80 (12.2)
1991	23.40 (12.3)	14.30 (18.7)	37.70 (14.1)
1997	26.11 (13.8)	19.09 (20.4)	46.37 (15.9)
1999	28.11 (14.5)	20.18 (23.0)	48.29 (17.2)
2000	28.57 (15.0)	20.66 (25.0)	49.23 (18.5)

Note: Figures in parentheses indicate percentage.

Source: *Yojana*, March 2003.

Women in Government Services

Participation of women in government services has been on increase while that of men is in the declining trend. Between the years 1981 and 1997 the employment of women in government services increased from 12 lakh to 16 lakh and in percentage terms it increased from 11 to 14.6 per cent. On the other hand the employment of men in percentage terms declined from 89 per cent to 83.4 per cent during the same period.

In the premier government services of IAS, IPS and IFS even though the participation of women is very low as against the dominance of men, but gradually it is in the increasing trend. These officers of the government from the years 1987 to 2000 is presented in Table 4.6.

Table 4.6

Women in Premier Government Services 1987-2000

Service	1987		1997		2000	
	No.	Per cent	No.	Per cent	No.	Per cent
IAS	339	7.5	512	10.2	535	10.4
IPS	21	0.9	67	2.2	110	3.3
IFS	53	10.0	71	12.0	n.a.	n.a.
Total	**413**	**5.80**	**650**	**7.5**	**645**	**7.6**

Source: Department of Personnel, Government of India, 2001.

The National Population Policy of Government of India, 2000 clearly recognises the importance of women's paid employment in achieving the goal of population stabilisation in the country and specified measures that will encourage paid-employment and self-employment for women. It has been recognised that the following five determinants of fertility directly or indirectly influences the stability of population. Of course all the variables are interrelated.

- Female workforce participation rate.
- Female literacy.
- Decision-making on women's own health care
- Earning and access to money.
- Use of family planning methods.

Employment of Married Women

In the country employment of married women is comparatively low. About 36 per cent of ever married women are employed in different jobs but about 26.2 per cent are doing jobs for cash earnings. In professional, technical and managerial job only 2 per cent of the married women are at work. About 11.4 per cent of married women employed earn pay equal to or more than their husbands.

The picture of married women in the states gives a diversified one. In Punjab and Haryana where the people are engaged in the developed form of agriculture and have comparatively higher per capita income among the states have very low percentage of married women, 8.9 and 9.7 per cent, employed for cash. Andhra Pradesh has highest per cent of married women employed for cash with 45.1 per cent. Out of 15 major states, in nine states the women employed for cash is lower to the national figure. Highest percentage of married women are working in professional jobs in Maharashtra and Kerala while Bihar has only less than one per cent of married women work for cash. Andhra Pradesh has highest percentage of married women who earn equal or more than the pay of their husbands, which double the figure of national figure.

Employment of ever married women in general and employed for cash, employment in professional jobs and per cent of women who earn equal or more than the salary of their husbands is presented in Table 4.7.

Table 4.7

Employed Married Women in the States of India, 2004

(Figures in per cent)

State	*Employed*	*Employed for cash*	*Professional, Technical, Managerial, jobs*	*More or equal to Husbands pay*
Haryana	12.6	9.7	2.7	4.1
Punjab	9.4	8.9	2.5	4.1
Rajasthan	45.3	14.9	1.5	8.5
Madhya Pradesh	57.2	31.6	2.0	13.8
Uttar Pradesh	23.4	10.6	1.2	4.1
Bihar	26.4	18.4	0.8	10.8
Orissa	30.6	25.9	1.5	9.6
West Bengal	28.5	25.4	1.5	13.0
Assam	20.2	18.1	1.8	9.3
Gujarat	50.8	31.6	2.3	10.7
Maharashtra	55.7	35.9	3.0	14.0
Andhra Pradesh	58.7	45.1	1.6	24.5
Karnataka	52.1	37.4	2.4	12.2
Kerala	25.0	22.3	3.8	9.8
Tamil Nadu	53.8	44.4	2.5	12.4
India	**39.1**	**26.2**	**2.0**	**11.4**

Source: *Economic and Political Weekly*, February 14, 2004.

Females in Main Workforce

Agriculture: In the main workforce 31.51 per cent are women workers. Agriculture continues to be a major field for women's employment. About 42.04 per cent of main women workers engaged in agricultural activities as cultivators and agricultural labourers. As cultivators the women form 20.10 per cent while as agricultural labourers they form 38.33 per cent. Nearly 63.70 per cent of all economically active men are engaged in agriculture, compared with 77.70 per cent of women.

Other Primary Sector: Live stock, forestry, fishing, hunting and other allied activities in the rural sector included in this category which marginally supplement the main agricultural work in earning some income to the family. In these activities 19 per cent of women are engaged and in total number of women workers 1.59 per cent are engaged in these activities.

Mining and Quarrying: In mining and quarrying the participation women is not at all significant. It is dominated by men workers to the magnitude of 87.59 per cent.

Manufacturing and Processing: The manufacturing and processing is again can be divided into two as: (a) household industry, and (b) other than household industry. In the household industry 32.92 per cent of women workers are involved while in other than household industry the percentage of participation is 11.27 per cent. After cultivation and agricultural labour the employment of women in the industrial sector is third in position; about 7.32 per cent of women workers are employed in this sector. Statistics do not, however, provide a complete picture of the work done by women, the hours of seasonal, part-time unpaid labour, apart from household work.

Construction: The construction sector is dominated by men workers. Women are generally work as helpers in unskilled work in the construction activities. Out of total female workers 5.99 per cent of women workers are employed in this sector.

Trade and Commerce: In this sector too men are in dominance in work. Only 6.82 per cent of workers are women in this sector and the rest of 93 per cent are men in this sector.

Transport and Communication: This sector engages mainly skilled workers and experts in different operational field hence the participation of women are of limited nature. The participation of women in this sector is least of all the industrial categories with only 2.60 per cent in the entire sector.

The overall sectoral employment of women in India shows that it is the private sector that employs highest percentage of eligible women in the jobs. The sector-wise composition of women employees in India in the four broad sectors of private, government, public sector and by the non-governmental organisations are presented in Fig.4.2 in a pie diagram below:

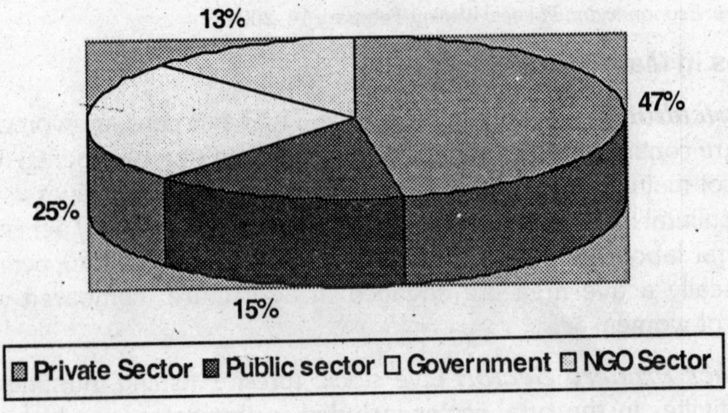

Fig.4.2: Employment of Women in Different Sectors of India

Wage Discrimination

There is discrimination of wages between men and women workers; this is mainly in the unorganised sectors. The gender wage discrimination is more in the rural agricultural sector than in the industrial sectors. Women engaged in agricultural operations, even though they are equally work along with the male workers, they are paid less traditionally taking them as inferior quality of work. In the urban sector especially in the construction sector the women workers are paid less for the specific work allotted to them or even for the same work done by the men.

Discrimination in wages is specific to India or to developing economies. A recent study shows (Assocham Study-2007, Women top in education: Why Miss top positions?) American women get paid 77 cents for every dollar earned by men. But it is found that 60 per cent of women are happy with their salaries. Women in the senior management posts are less than males; the highest percentage of women in the top management posts is found in Philippines with 97 per cent followed by China with 91 per cent. And in comparison to that India has only have women in top management post with 56 per cent. (International Business Report, 2007, Grant Thornton, *Women in Management*) Women are not able to reach in the top level managerial posts due to several reasons; the main reasons found in a study reveals that 42 per cent of women find no time to look into the job positions available in the managerial post. Next to it women are reluctant to move places to get top jobs and also change jobs frequently.

Table 4.8 shows three important reasons for women which hold them back to move to the top most managerial posts, even if they are offered for it.

Table 4.8

Reasons for Backing of Women for Top Managerial Post

Rank	*Reason*	*Per cent*
1	Lack of time (for networking, etc.)	42.00
2	Reluctant to change (from jobs or locations)	34.66
3	Family responsibilities	16.67
	Others	6.67
	Total	**100.00**

Source: Assocham Study-2007, Women top in Education: Why miss top positions?

Number of persons employed in the different industrial categories in India with male and female breakout and per cent of female workers in each category for the year 1991 is presented in Table 4.9.

Table 4.9

Proportion of Women Workers by Industrial Categories

(Figures in '000)

Category of Workers	*Male*	*Female*	*Per cent of Female Workers*
Cultivators	856	215	20.10
Agricultural workers	455	283	38.33
Other Primary activities	43	10	19.00
Mining and quarrying	15	2	12.41
Manufacturing processing	137	46	16.19
Construction	50	4	7.71
Trade and Commerce	193	14	6.82
Transport and communication	76	2	2.60
Others	233	52	18.21
Total	**2058**	**628**	**30.51**

Source: Census of India, 1991.

The composition of female workers in different industrial categories is shown in a pie diagram in Fig.4.3.

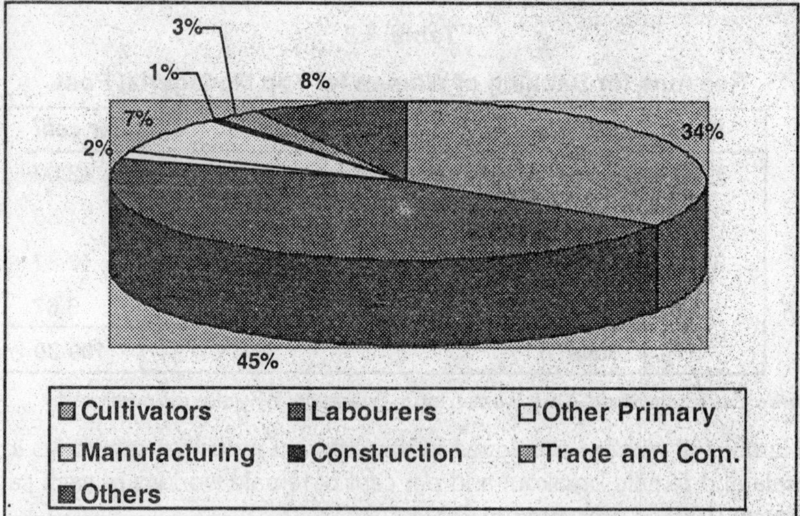

Fig.4.3: Composition of Female Workers by Industrial Category

Work Participation of Women in Orissa

Development and modernization have helped the women worldover to come out of the family, to participate in market process as workers, managers, employees and so on. In fact wage work has been used as a tool to remove gender imbalance. The neo-classical theorist stated that women have lower productivity than men, because of their lower level of human capital, viz., education, training, on job experience and therefore they earn less. Even today for a developing country like India it holds good.

Table 4.9 shows wide disparity between men and women in labour market of Orissa. In comparison to male workers participation the female workers form about only 24.62 per cent in the year 2001 as against 52.75 per cent for males. This is far from satisfactory in case of female workers. Of course, it is found that the growth of female workers over the period of 30 years has increased by 138 per cent but on the other hand the rate of work participation reduced marginally for male workers by about 2.87 per cent.

Table 4.9

Male and Female Workers in Orissa

Year	*Male*	*Female*	*Total*
1961	60.75	26.58	43.66
1971	55.62	10.47	33.19
1981	55.86	19.81	38.01
1991	53.79	20.79	37.53
2001	52.75	24.62	38.88

Source: Census of India 2001.

Organised Sector

Employment in organized industry has done much to draw women out of the family and household, which had hitherto made-up their world. The wages earned through industrial employment has given them a measure of independence, besides contributing handsomely to household earning. It gives them a degree of confidence, and a sense of self-respect.

The proportion of women employees in the organised sector shows an increasing trend but is very marginal. Out of 7.67 lakh employees in the organised sector during 2003; women employees account for 13.8 per cent as against 13.4 per cent during 2002. During the last five years the number of women employees in the public sector has increased from 83,045 to 95,644 showing an increase of 15.2 per cent, on the other hand the women employees in the private sector during 1999 was 10,322 which declined to 10,140 in 2003 showing a decline of 1.8 per cent. The specific figures are shown in Table 4.10.

Table 4.10

Women Employment in Organised Sector: Orissa

(Figures in lakh)

Year	Public Sector		Private Sector		Total Organised Sector		Per cent of Women to Total Employees
	Total	Women	Total	Women	Total	Women	
1999	7.09	0.83	0.93	0.10	8.02	0.93	11.65
2000	7.11	0.89	0.87	0.10	7.98	0.99	12.41
2001	7.17	0.92	0.89	0.10	8.06	1.02	12.63
2002	6.92	0.93	0.79	0.10	7.71	1.03	13.38
2003	6.80	0.96	0.87	0.10	7.67	1.06	13.78

Source: Economic Survey 2004-05 Government of Orissa, Bhubaneswar.

The socio-economic status of women in the state of Orissa is characterized by low female literacy, distressing health and nutritional deficiencies and the declining trend of sex ratio. In order to mitigate these problems, women development has been given a prominent place in the agenda of development activities of the state.

Women in Workforce

According to 2001 Census, only 31.2 per cent of the total workforce in Orissa is women. The main workers and marginal workers among females constitute about 34.93 per cent and 65.07 per cent of the total female workers respectively. The unorganized primary sector, which includes agriculture, animal husbandry, fishery, forestry, mining and quarrying, plantation and allied activities, absorbs as much as 73.8 per cent of the total female workers. Women constitute an important segment of labour force. The unpaid economic activities of women and their contribution in the domestic sector remain unreported and go largely unorganized.

Agriculture and Allied Activities

Women play an important role in the primary sector of the state's economy. According to 2001 census, 73.8 percent of the female work force was engaged in agriculture, 19.4 per cent as cultivators and 54.4 per cent as agricultural workers generally participate in all operations except ploughing. A large number of female workers are also engaged in marginal occupation such as collection of fish, firewood, cow dung, fetching drinking water, maintenance of kitchen garden tailoring weaving etc. in order to supplement the family income.

Occupational Structure:

Among the four categories of workers agriculture occupies the pivotal place in the share of employment for both men and women. The Census classifies workers into four broad categories, viz.: (1) cultivator, (2) agricultural labour, (3) household industries, (4) other workers.

Sex ratio of workers as cultivator, agricultural labourer, household industries and other workers is presented in Table 4.11. There has been a faster increase in sex ratio of cultivator from 46 to 204. However, agricultural labourer continue to share the highest rates.

Table 4.11

Sex Ratio of Different Categories of Workers in Orissa

Categories	*Sector*	*1971*	*1981*	*1991*	*2001*
Cultivator	Total	46	92	122	204
	Rural	46	92	123	206
	Urban	46	71	_	115
Agricultural Labourers	Total	252	462	542	484
	Rural	252	467	544	486
	Urban	253	385	384	386
Household Industries	Total	317	386	418	550
	Rural	330	403	412	568
	Urban	202	277	255	346
Other Workers	Total	101	129	172	181
	Rural	139	141	_	207
	Urban	101	112	_	132

Source: Census of India, 1971 to 2001.

Programmes for Women Employment

There are number of important programmes now implemented by the Government of India to provide employment and self-employment opportunities to the women which are briefly analyzed in the following:

(1) Mission Shakti:

Mission Shakti, is a self-help mission for empowering women. It was launched in the state in March 2001. Under Mission Shakti 1,61,386 Self-help Groups (SHG) have been formed with more than 20 lakh women as members. Four state level trade based associations of women have been formed under Mission Shakti of the producer of turmeric powder, leaf cup plates, handicrafts, phenyl and chalk. More than Rs.43 crore has been advanced to about 1,47 thousand SHGs by various banks as credit. These women self-help groups are engaged in different types of economic activities such as horticulture, piggery, goatary, diary and other economic activities.

(2) Swasakti Project:

The Rural Women's Development and Empowerment Project rechristened as Swasakti Project in 1998 and being implemented in nine states of Bihar, Chhattisghad, Gujarat, Haryana, Jharkhand, Karnataka, Madhya Pradesh, Uttaranchal and Uttar Pradesh. The projects aims at enhancing women's access to resources for better quality of life through the use of drudgery and time reduction devises, health, literacy and imparting skills for confidence building and income generating activities. So, for 17,647 SHGs have been formed under this project. The project is supported jointly by the, World Bank and International Fund for Agricultural Development (IFAD).

(3) Swayamsiddha (Self-empowerment):

A programme for women's empowerment known as "Swayamsiddha" has been introduced during the year 2001-2002 through Self-help Groups (SHG) with emphasis on covering services, developing access to micro-credit and promoting micro-enterprises. The important component of this programme is formulation, implementation and monitoring of block specific projects for five years though the Project Implementation Agency (PIA). This can also be implemented through suitable non-government organisations approved by the state governments. So far, more then fifty thousand SHGs have been formed in the 650 blocks of the country.

In Orissa this programme is being implemented in the 36 blocks of Kalahandi-Bolangir-Koraput (KBK) districts and in one backward districts of Boudh. The programme aims for economic upliftment and other socio-economic issues, strengthening and institutionalizing the saving habit of rural women and their control over economic resources and improving access of women to institutional credit.

(4) Training and Extension in Agriculture:

Training and extension for women in agriculture (TEWA) project had been implemented since 1987 in Orissa with assistance from DANIDA with a view to increasing agricultural productivity and income of women farmers. It had been operating in eight undivided districts namely Puri, Ganjam, Bolangir, Keonjhir, Koraput, Sambalpur and Sundergarh. Under the project 1160 farm women groups were formed and 36,772 farm women were trained during 2000-03.

(5) Support to Training and Employment Programme for Women: (STEP):

This programme provides update skills and new knowledge to poor asset-less women in eight traditional sectors of employment namely, agriculture, animal husbandry, dairying, fisheries, handlooms, handicrafts, Khadi and Village Industries and seri-culture. The scheme is being implemented through public sector organisations, state corporations, cooperatives and voluntary organisations which existed at least three years experience. So far, eleven projects have been sanctioned to benefit more than 16 thousand women in various sectors.

(6) Swabalamban (Self-reliance):

This scheme aims to provide training and skills to women to facilitate them to obtain employment or self-employment on a sustainable basis. Some of the trades where the training is imparted are computer programming, medical transcription, electronic assembling, radio and television repairs, garment making, handloom weaving, handicrafts, secretarial practice, community health work and embroidery. There are 463 approved proposals under the scheme which benefited 17,240 women since 2003-04.

(7) Day Care Centres for Children and Working Mothers:

This programme aims to provide day care service to children for the age group of 0-5 years of parents whose income does not exceed Rs. 1,800 per month. Facilities provide to children are sleeping and day care facilities, supplementary nutrition, immunization, medicine and recreation. The scheme is being implemented by the three national level organizations, namely: (1) Central Social Welfare Bard, (2) the Indian Council for Child Welfare, and (3) Bharatiya Adim Jati Sevak Sangh. So far, about 33.11 lakh children are benefited under the scheme.

(8) Swadhar:

This scheme was launched in 2001-02 for providing holistic and integrated services to women in difficult circumstances. The package of services made available under this scheme includes provision of food, clothing, shelter, health care counselling and legal supports. So far, 31 projects are being funded under the scheme. The following are some of the benefits provided under this scheme:

(1) Destitute widows deserted by their families in religious places like Vrindavan and Kashi.

(2) Women prisoners released from jail and without family support,

(3) Women survivors of natural disasters who have been rendered homeless and without social and economic support,

(4) Trafficked women rescued or run away from brothels and other places or victims of sexual crimes who are disowned by their families or those do not want to go back to their respective families.

(9) Rashtriya Mahila Kosh (National Credit Fund):

This credit fund was set-up as a registered society in the year 1993 with a view to facilitate credit support to poor women to start income generating activities such as in dairy, agriculture, shopkeeping, vending and handicrafts. Annually around 20 thousand women are being benefited under this scheme. In the year 2003-04 alone, more than 32 thousand women were benefited.

(10) Mahila Vikas Samabaya Nigam:

The Mahila Vikas Samabaya Nigam (MVSN) is the nodal agency at state-level for empowerment of women. It has 217 affiliated societies and the remaining 163 are registered under the Societies Registration Act, 1860. As a state nodal agency, the Nigam undertakes activities in three categories namely, economic programmes, social sensitization programmes and allied infrastructural activities. The MVSN undertakes various training programmes for women for capacity building in order to enable them to take-up different income generating activities. The types of training programmes conducted are Entrepreneurship Development Programme, Training on marketing and sales promotion and other special training programmes for women. Besides trade-based technical training programmes are also conducted in non-traditional sector, such as woollen carpet weaving, fancy leather, ragzin bags, gems and American diamond cutting, polishing and other activities. Under Norwegian Assistance for development of women (NORAD) scheme an amount of Rs. 361.86 lakh was sanctioned in 148 cases and 7,210 beneficiaries benefited by the end of 2002-03.

The government has taken several steps to promote women's employment and welfare in these directions:

- training women in non-traditional areas, particularly linked to agriculture and non-farm base scheme;
- improvement in the conditions of women working in the informal agricultural sector;
- provision for the direct access to the institutional credit, and
- Affirmative actions to ensure women have access to educational opportunities to increase possibilities of wage employment and support services.

Government claims sufficient achievements in the schemes for women but in fact there are several lacunas in the implementation of the programmes and the targets have not been reached as desired. The government has been collaborating with the NGOs in the various women development schemes to provide the services to the target groups but achievements are not satisfactory.

Hostel for Working Women:

Even though women get jobs but most important problem for them is joining the job at a distance place and availability of suitable accommodation to live in. That is why the parents of the girls also reluctant to send them to distance places for work and remain single. Hostels for working women scheme were launched as far back as in 1972 to overcome this difficulty. Under this scheme financial assistance is provided to NGOs taking up of women's activities, cooperative bodies, public sector undertakings, local bodies and universities the construction of hostels for working women. Hostel accommodation also provided to women taking training courses for employment and girl students studying in post-school professional courses.

✻✻✻

Chapter 5 MICROFINANCE AND WOMEN

In the middle of 1980s the concept of microfinance was developed and experimented by Mahamad Yonus of Grameen (Rural) Bank of Bangladesh with the assistance provided by World Bank. He had organised the rural poor women into small groups of ten to twenty members, trained them in the art of savings and provided small amounts of loan to the needy women in the group without the use of collateral security; introduced the concept of microfinance, which now popularly known as "Self-Help Group" (SHG) stimulated the development of microfinance movement all over the world.

Characteristics of the SHG

The SHG is a small economically homogeneous group of rural women with the main characterises:

- The members of the group create a common fund by their own regular contribution, which is saved in the bank.
- Loan request of the individual members considered and approved by the group in-group meetings for the individual needs.
- Loan is given on trust with a minimum documentation of the details without any security.
- The loan amount is small, frequent and for short duration with usual rate of bank interest.

Models of the SHGs

There are three models of the SHGs functioning in India in the different states:

1. ***First Model:*** These SHGs are formed and financed directly by the Commercial and Rural Regional Banks.

2. ***Second Model:*** These SHGs are formed by the NGOs, different government departments and agencies but directly financed by the local banks.
3. ***Third Model:*** In this model the bank finance the SHGs that is formed by the NGOs and the bank accept NGOs as the financial intermediary.

The SHG in India

In 1970s many NGOs in India began experiments in microfinance to tackle poverty issues and create self-employment opportunity for women. In 1986-87 the NABARD financed an action-oriented research on savings and credit management of the SHG of an NGO in Karnataka. In 1988-89 the NABARD took a study of functioning of the SHGs to examine the possibility of mobilisation of rural savings and improve the delivery of credit to poor women. In 1991 the RBI in a circular advised the commercial and cooperative banks to make the SHG operations a part of the normal banking business. In 1994 the RBI further advised the banks to treat lending to the SHG under the priority sector advances.

By the end of 2004-05 there are 11.45 lakh SHGs in the country. The growth rate was highest in 1999-2000 with more than 248 per cent, even though afterwards the absolute figure with SHGs shown good increase, in percentage terms the growth rate has been declined since 1999-2000. The figure of growth of SHGs from 1998-99 to 2004-05 is shown in Table 5.1.

Table 5.1

Growth of SHGs in India

Year	*No. in lakh*	*Growth*	*Growth Per cent*	*Loan Disbursed Rs. Crore*
1994-95	0.02	—	—	2.45
1995-96	0.05	3	150	6.06
1996-97	0.09	4	80	11.84
1997-98	0.14	5	55	23.79
1998-99	0.33	19	135	52.06
1999-00	1.15	82	248	150.13
2000-01	2.64	149	130	400.75
2001-02	4.61	197	75	699.75
2002-03	7.17	256	56	1088.33
2003-04	9.27	210	30	1407.09
2004-05	11.45	218	26	1737.99

Source: Kisan World, Vol. 33, No. 2, Feb. 2006, NABARD, 2006.

In the country the southern region dominants in number of SHGs; there are 9.39 lakh groups in the region, which forms about 82 per cent of the total SHGs in the country. The Andhra Pradesh tops in organising the women SHGs where 98.79 per cent of the total number of SHGs in the state are a women group. Kerala follows this with 95.73 and Tamil Nadu with 91.50 per cent. But in percentage terms the women SHGs are highest in eastern region with 89.93 per cent of women's groups. The regional-wise figures are shown in Table 5.2.

Table 5.2

Regional-wise Percentage of Women's SHGs

Region	*Percentage of Women Groups*
Eastern Region	89.93
Western Region	82.44
Central Region	72.01
Southern Region	74.24

It was evolved as an effective system for provision of financial services to the poor households, more specifically micro-enterprises. Internationally several variants of microfinance technologies have evolved in the last two decades. It refers to small-scale financial services for both credits and deposits that are provided to people for–

1. Operation of small farms, fishponds and rearing of livestock.
2. Operate small or micro-enterprises where goods are produced, repaired, recycled, and traded,
3. Provide services, work for wages or commissions, and gain income from renting out small amounts of land, vehicles, draft animals, or machinery tools, to other individuals and local groups.

Types of Microfinance

Broadly, the microfinance system could be classified into five groups according to the nature of operation of finance:

I. Grameen and Solidarity Model:

This model consists of a group of people, three to eight persons, on the condition that each of them would be assuming responsibility for the lending and all other financial operations. Lending as well as repayment is made directly to and from the individuals with the guarantee of the other group members. Grameen Bank of Bangladesh has perfected this procedure and it has been adopted in many countries with modifications to suit local conditions and cultures. The programmes of Banco Sol in Bolivia and most of the solidarity group models in Latin America follow this methodology (Sinha 2005).

II. The Group Approach:

In the group approach the entire financial process is delegated to the group rather than to the financial institutions. Savings, loans, loan repayments are taken care of at the group level. These groups are in turn linked to financial or micro-finance institutions for sourcing additional funds as well as depositing their savings. In India the organisation of Self Help Group (SHG) is very popular along with the Bank Linkage Programme. The PHBK project in Indonesia and the Chikola groups of K-REP in Kenya are the best examples of this technology.

III. Individual Credit:

Credit given directly to the individuals also forms a part of the microfinance technology. Many institutions have adopted the individual credit route for micro-finane where loan appraisal, loan disbursements and loan repayments are all done in an individual basis. Best examples of this type of technology are BRI – Unit Desa in Indonesia as well as priority sector lending by banks in India — especially the Regional Rural Banks (RRBs) and Cooperative Banks.

IV. Community Banking:

According to this methodology basic financial necessities of the poor especially women are met through the community banking system. The community village banks are organized with 30-50 members. These banks in turn borrow from the programme implementing institution and lend-on to the members. The village bank of FINCA in Latin America, which had been replicated in Africa and Central Asia are the best examples of this methodology.

V. Credit Unions and Cooperatives:

These institutions provide credit and other financial services to their members. The apex bodies provide technical and financial support to the federating units. The SANASA of Sri Lanka is a successful example of rural credit cooperative as microfinance service provider (Das and Satish 2000).

Microfinance in India

Microfinance institution started in India in 1980s through Self Help Groups (SHGs) model. It is the Grameen replication model of Bangladesh. The beginning was made with the initiative of NABARD's pilot project in Karnataka (1986-87) by linking SHGs with formal banks, mediating through NGOs. The NABARD undertook a survey of 43 NGOs in 11 states in India to study the functioning of microfinance, SHGs and their collaboration possibilities with the formal banking system. A pilot project for linking SHGs with banks was launched by the NABARD in 1992. The Reserve Bank of India persuaded Commercial Banks, Regional Rural Banks and Cooperative Banks to actively participate in the linkage programme. The SHG-bank linkage project was expected to be advantageous to the banking sector from both angles of fulfilment of social goals and achieving operational efficiency. The growth of SHG-bank linkage programme is presented in Table 5.1. In the initial period in 1992-93 just 255 SHGs were linked to banks with Rs. 2.98 million as refinance from the NABARD. In 2000-01 it rapidly expanded linking 2,34,843 SHGs and refinancing of Rs. 4,007.46 million. The SHG-bank linkage programme covered 412 districts in 25 states and two union territories.

Table 5.1

Growth of SHG-Bank Linkage Programme 1992-2001

Year	*Cumulative*	
	No. of Groups	*Amount of Loan (Rs. in Million)*
1992-93	255	2.89
1993-94	620	6.53
1994-95	2122	24.45
1995-96	4757	60.58
1996-97	8598	118.36
1997-98	14317	237.95
1998-99	32995	520.60
1999-00	114775	1501.26
2000-01	234843	4007.46

Source: NABARD, 2002.

The access to microfinance services (credit, savings, insurance and pensions) is still highly unequal between men and women. Considerable advances were made in the 1990s in the design of NGO-managed programmes and poverty-targeted banks to increase women's access to small loans and savings facilities. Literature prepared for the Micro-credit Summit Campaign presents an extremely attractive vision of increasing numbers of expanding microfinance programmes which not only give many women access to microfinance services, but also initiate a 'virtuous upward spiral' of empowerment (Mayoux 1998). This optimism about the implicit empowerment potential of credit and savings pervades most donor statements on microfinance. Donors and NGOs tend to expand their microfinance activities generally rather than support more explicitly empowerment-focussed interventions for women. At the same time, microfinance is being promoted as a key poverty alleviation strategy to enable poor women and men to cope with the adverse economic and social impacts of structural adjustment policies and globalisation (Mayoux 2001).

The Micro Credit Summit Campaign reports that 14.2 million of the world's poorest women now have access to financial services accounting for nearly 74% of the 19.3 million poorest served by microfinance. Sinapi Aba Trust (SAT) in Ghana recognized that most of the women are empowered through microfinance. Women's empowerment project in Nepal showed 68% of women experienced an increase in their decision-making role in the areas of family planning, children's marriage, buying and selling and sending their daughters to school. World education found that the combination of education and credit put women in a stronger position to ensure more equal access for female children to food, schooling and medical care. It is found that women's financial contributions helped them greater respect from their husband and children, negotiate husband's help with housework, and avoid family quarrels over money. It is also found increased respect from and better relationships with extended family and laws. Hashmi and Schuler found a reduced incidence of violence among women who were members of credit organizations than among the general population. Working Women's Forum in India (WWF) found 41% of its members who had experienced domestic violence were able to stop it due to personal empowerment, and 29% were able to stop it through group action (www.ilo.org).

The World Bank reports that societies that discriminate on the basis of gender have greater poverty, slower economic growth, weaker governance, and a lower standard of living (World Bank 2001). Studies in Latin America and elsewhere show that men typically contribute 50 to 60 per cent of their salaries to the collective household fund, whereas women "tend to keep nothing back for themselves" because, "women contribute decisively to the well-being of their families".

Every microfinance institution has stories of women who not only are better off economically, as a result of access to credit, but are empowered as well. Simply getting cash into the hands of women (by way of working capital) can lead to increased self-esteem, control and empowerment by helping them to achieve greater economic independence and security, which in turn gives them the chance to contribute financially to their households and communities (www.microcreditsummit.org).

Microfinance and Women Empowerment

There are four basic views on the link between microfinance and women's empowerment:

- There are those who stress the positive evidence and are essentially optimistic about the possibility of sustainable microfinance programmes worldwide empowering women;
- Another school of thought recognizes the limitations to empowerment, but explains those with poor programme design;
- Others recognize the limitations of microfinance for promoting empowerment, but see it as a key ingredient as important in themselves within a strategy to alleviate poverty; empowerment in this view needs to be addressed by other means;
- Then there are those who see microfinance programmes as a waste of resources.

From the early 1970s, women's movements in a number of countries identified credit as a major constraint on women's ability to earn an income and became increasingly interested in the degree to which poverty-focussed credit women were actually using programmes and credit cooperatives. SEWA in India, for example, set-up credit programmes as part of a multipronged strategy for an organization of informal sector women workers. Since the 1970s, many women's organizations worldwide have included credit and savings, both as a way of increasing women's incomes and to bring women together to address wider gender issues. The 1980s saw the emergence of poverty-targeted microfinance institutions like Grameen Bank and ACCION and others. Many of these programmes see themselves as empowerment-oriented. In the 1990s, a combination of evidence of high female repayment rates and the rising influence of gender lobbies within donor agencies and NGOs led to increasing emphasis on targeting women in microfinance programmes (Mayoux 2001).

Microfinance is now a proven strategy for reaching poor women. Within the family, poverty strikes women disproportionately hard. They are the poorest among the poorer section with limited access to resources. Though the face of poverty is changing, the poverty of women continues to remain a constant factor. There is continued inequality and vulnerability of women in all sectors economic, social, political, educational, legal, health care and nutrition. As the women are oppressed in all spheres of life, they need to be empowered in all walks of life. Women need to be empowered for gaining collective strength. Collective strength is necessary for building solidarity and support among themselves to achieve empowerment (Manimekalai 2004).

One of the important reasons for the underdevelopment of women is their non-involvement in income generating activities and their economic dependence. In the past, the women depended on local moneylenders to meet their financial needs during marriages, illness and other emergency conditions. During these crucial times the moneylenders exploited them by charging exorbitant interest rates. Though financial institutions were available, it was difficult for them to have direct contact with these institutions. Lack of awareness, cumbersome lending procedure, inadequate supervision, defective loans policies and procedures, misutilisation of loans, inability to link credit with marketing, non-recognition of the need for consumption, finance and ineffective credit supervision, etc., are the main shortcomings of rural financial institutions.

To bridge the gap between demand and supply of funds in the lower lungs of the rural economy, the microfinance sector took initiative to develop a supplementary credit delivery mechanism by encouraging institutional arrangement outside the financial system. In this connection, microfinance institution is started as a Grameen model in Bangladesh. During seventies several developing countries in Asia and Latin America took initiative in this regard. India has also adopted this system by suitable modifications in accordance with its socio-economic and political conditions. With the launching of NABARD's pilot scheme to cure the illness of rural poverty gained concepts like self-reliance, self-sufficiency and self-help as its core. It helped the rural women in starting up their Income Generating Activities (IGA) or micro-enterprise through Self Help Groups (SHGs) (Patro 2002).

There are basically two schools of thought on the empowerment potential of microfinance programmes, with one school emphasizing the negative aspects, arguing that men in the households tend to appropriate the loans and benefits from the loans. This school sees the households as a site of conflict, where women and men are struggling to control over resources. The other school emphasizes the positive aspects, given the evidence that households with loans generally have higher incomes and levels of consumption, regardless of the gender dynamics within the households. This school emphasizes a more consensual conception of the households, with benefits for entire family also considered as benefit to women.

Some Positive Facts

1. ***Women's ability to make decisions:*** There is evidence of increased decision-making, including decision about business investments. At times, the step forward implies joint decision-making with their husbands instead of previously no involvement at all. A limitation is that the increased decision-making on household matters often has been limited to more traditional, female stereotype areas of decision-making.

2. ***Increased self-confidence:*** It is difficult to measure. Evidence was strongest when the provision of microfinance was linked with additional activities such as knowledge provision, providing women with opportunity to participate in discussions on social and legal issues.

3. ***Status and domestic violence:*** Some men confirmed having difficulty to adopt new roles. Women tend to report that relationships have improved through; there is little evidence of changes of gender roles. Some studies point at a backlash effect, increased domestic violence, as women challenge gender norms and assert their rights. Overall evidence is of improved family relationships. There is also anecdotal evidence of reduced violence against women and children. So, on the whole there is little evidence that microfinance is destroying families. Women in fact seek to strengthen their relative position within an independent relationship with their husbands than seeking independence and autonomy.

4. ***Status in the community:*** There have been evidences of improved status in the community, higher mobility and viability.

5. ***Economic empowerment:*** Households with loans are better-off in terms of income and consumption pattern than those without. Women tend to spend the benefits on family welfare, food, health and school fees, and less on investments into their own business. The education of girls increases in households where women have taken a loan.

6. ***Political empowerment:*** Little evidence of political empowerment as an outcome of microfinance programmes. However, it can provide opportunities to gain leadership experience and confidence. Some organizations include training programmes or have a union and advocacy branch (SEWA-India) along side the credit programmes, and these have impacted on political and legal empowerment. For example, Fatima Bi of Kalva village in Andhra Pradesh, who is unlettered and had never seen a city, became a Sarpanch of the village through reservation under the Panchayat legislation, and in 2003, she received UN award from the Secretary General, for her work in terms of poverty alleviation. Similarly, Sudha Patel, a 21-year-old blind girl of Changa Village in Gujarat, became a Sarpanch in spite of her handicap, and went to win the outstanding Women Panchayat Leader Award at Delhi in 2003 (Patro 2002).

Some Limitations

1. ***Burden of meetings:*** Time consuming meetings, in particular in programmes based on group lending, and time-consuming income generating activities without reduction of traditional responsibilities increase women's work and time burden.
2. ***New pressures:*** By using social capital, in group lending/group collateral programmes, additional stresses and pressures are introduced, which might increase vulnerability and reflect disempowerment.
3. ***Reinforcement of traditional gender roles:*** Microfinance assists women to perform traditional roles better and women thus remain trapped in low productivity sectors, not moving from the group of survival enterprises to micro-enterprises to micro-entrepreneurship. There is evidence of men withdrawing their contributions to certain type of household expenditures.

Factors that Contribute to Empowerment:

1. ***Gender sensitive programmes:*** Employment of gender sensitive staff, female loan officer, taking into account women's life cycle and time schedules is the need of the hour. There is a need to increase women's leadership in MFIs.
2. ***Credit with business training:*** Business training, training in planning costs calculations, marketing enhance women's ability to make effective use of microfinance services.
3. ***Credit with general education:*** General education, literacy, skill development, health, family planning contributes to women's overall well-being and commitment to educate their children and daughters.
4. ***Social and political issues:*** Contribute to sense of solidarity among women and knowledge of their rights and to include men, orienting

them to new gender roles, and need for new balances in family and work responsibilities.

Microfinance Schemes for Women

Rashtriya Mahila Kosh (RMK)

RMK sponsored by Government of India (Department of Women and Child Development) was set-up in 1993 with the objective of assisting women below the poverty line in undertaking income generating activities through provision of package, financial and other services and encourage promotion of women in SHGs. Its head office is in New Delhi. Microfinance as is being practised by Rashtriya Mahila Kosh (RMK), could be defined as a set of services comprising following activities: a) Micro-credit – small loans, primarily for income generating activities, but also for consumption and contingency needs, b) Micro-savings- thrift or small savings from borrowers own resources (Nagayya 2000). The main function of RMK is to provide credit for facilitating production and economic activities, along with some support for training for skill upgradation.

The main features of the microfinance service being provided by RMK are: It is a tool for empowerment of the poorest, the higher the income and better the asset position of the borrower, the lower the incremental benefit from the micro-credit. Delivery is normally through Self-help Groups (SHGs). It is essentially for promoting self-employment, as the opportunities of wage employment are limited in developing countries. Microfinance increases the productivity of self-employment in the informal sector of the economy – generally used for: (a) direct income generation, (b) management of assets and liabilities for the household to participate in future opportunities, and (c) consumption smoothing.

Mahila Vikash Nidhi (MVN)

MVN is specially designed for economic empowerment of women. Training and employment opportunities are provided to them through creation of necessary infrastructure. Besides supply of improved inputs, production and technological improvements are also covered under the MVN scheme. The progress of this scheme has been noteworthy. By March 1997, 113 NGOs supported benefiting over 14,000 women with an aggregate assistance of Rs. 499.69 lakh (RASS 1998).

Rashtriya Grameen Vikash Nidhi (RGVN)

It is established in 1990 with headquarters at Guwahati (Assam) as a non-profit society. Its sponsors are IFCI, IDBI and NABARD. RGVN aims to improve the quality of life of the poor or otherwise underprivileged rural and urban people through social action. Micro-Credit Programmes also known as Credit and Savings Programmes (CSP) was launched by RGVN in May 1995. NABARD and SIDBI are providing support to this programme. RGVN extends financial and tech-managerial supports to NGOs with a view to empowering them to implement income-generating activities for the poor.

Purpose of Loans

The individual members the SHGs generally avail loan for six purposes as mentioned in Table 5.3. Since the all-India figures of nature of loan are not available, figures are obtained from two separate studies in Tamil Nadu and Orissa for a comparative view. Tamil Nadu is a comparatively advanced state and Orissa is a backward state.

Tamil Nadu: In this state about two-thirds of loan availed for productive purpose of agriculture and business investment. Agriculture tops with 42.92 per cent of loan followed by business with 24.04 per cent in the second position. About 33 per cent of loan availed for unproductive purposes, which comprises loan taken for festival expenses, daily consumption expenses and repayment of loans.

Orissa: In this state the productive loans form about 36.57 per cent and rest is for unproductive purpose. The first position forms consumption loan, which is 41.21 per cent, followed by agriculture and allied purpose in the second position with 25 per cent. In repayment of loan the Orissa women resorted to less than Tamil women with only 10.82 per cent but the latter about 16 per cent. Orissan women taken more loans for marriages and other festival functions than Tamilian and it is found that the Orissan women incurred loan for the purpose of medical treatment, which is not found with the Tamil women.

Table 5.3

Purpose of Loan Availed by SHG Members

(Figures in per cent)

Purpose of loan	*Tamil Nadu*	*Orissa*
Agriculture and allied activities	42.92	25.00
Business investment	24.03	11.57
Repayment of loan	16.03	10.82
Consumption loan	13.39	41.21
Marriage and social functions	3.63	5.83
Health and medical	0	5.57
	100	**100**

Source: Ph.D. thesis P. Dhavamani, Madurai Kamaraj University, Madurai for Tamil Nadu, 2006 and M.Phil. thesis of Ananta Basudeb Sahu, Brahmapur University for Orissa, 2005.

Benefits from the SHG

In an opinion poll taken in Orissa by a scholar it is found that the members of the different groups are very much satisfied with the operation of the group and expressed that they are benefited very much in several aspects. In seven items of the benefit posed as question the response of group members is very encouraging.

Since many SHGs are taken as sample for the opinion poll and expressed different percentages in Table 5.4 the maximum response and the range of opinion is presented for a quick observation. The respondent women felt that since they joined the group there was considerable increase in their self-confidence as maximum of 86.88 per cent of women felt it. Social cohesion and habit of savings improvement felt about 80 per cent in the second position. About 75 per cent felt that they are now free from debt trap, while 70 per cent expressed now they are in a beter position as far as the economic independence is concerned. In employment generation and acquiring of assets they are in the last position but about 58 per cent, which seems satisfactory.

Table 5.4

Benefits Derived by the SHG Members

(Figures in per cent)

Benefits	*Maximum Per cent*	*Range of Benefits Felt derived in Per cent*
Self-confidence	86.86	78.00 - 86.86
Social cohesion	80.88	68.88 – 80.88
Saving habits	80.66	68.22 – 80.66
Freedom from debt	75.08	49.00 – 75.08
Economic independence	70.00	65.00 – 70.00
Employment	58.90	21.11 – 58.90
Asset ownership	58.22	24.40 – 58.22

Source: M.Phil. thesis of Ananta Basudeb Sahu, Brahmapur University, Orissa, 2005.

Income Generation

One of the main objectives of development of the SHGs is generation of extra income for the members of the SHG. Income of the member of the SHG before joining and after the joining the SHG shows quite encouraging. The main findings of income generation are:

- The range of income generation increased from Rs. 1,200 to Rs. 2,000, an increase of about 66.67 per cent.
- About 33 per cent of the members earned more than what they were earning maximum of Rs. 1,200 earlier and added Rs. 3.07 lakh to their individual families.
- Total earnings of the women's income increased from Rs.4.39 lakh to Rs.6.55 lakh, an increase of 49.20 per cent, after they joined the SHGs.
- At the lowest level of 8.67 per cent of women earned below Rs. 300 but after joining in the SHGs now 9.33 per cent of them earning below Rs. 500 increasing their total income to Rs. 0.14 lakh.

- Earlier the highest number of 39.67 per cent of women in the income range of Rs. 601-900 earned Rs. 1.78 lakh, but after joining the SHGs the women with the income range of Rs. 500-1,000 with 34.67 per cent of women earning Rs. 1.56 lakhs.

The income earning of 600 women in different SHGs their earliar income and income after their joining of the SHGs presented in Table 5.5.

Saving Habits

Before joining the SHGs the 69.23 of the women were not at all saving any thing but after joining all of them are now saving accounts and regularly saving. In pre-SHG days the savings were only Rs. 5,396, which comes to Rs. 30 on an average per women member. But in post-SHG days the total savings increased to Rs. 18,762 by all the members of the SHGs, but on the average per women member the savings are almost remain same, marginally increased to Rs. 32 of course the total savings increased shows an increase of 248 per cent.

Table 5.5

Income Before and After Joining the SHGs

Income before Joining the Group				*Income after Joining the Group*			
Range of Income Rs.	*No.*	*Per cent*	*Rs. lakh*	*Range of Income Rs.*	*No.*	*Per cent*	*Rs. lakh*
< 300	52	8.67	0.08	<500	56	9.33	0.14
300-600	126	21.0	0.57	501-1000	208	34.67	1.56
601-900	238	39.67	1.78	1001-1500	142	23.67	1.78
901-1200	166	27.66	1.74	1501-2000	128	21.33	2.24
>1200	18	3.00	0.22	>2000	66	11.00	0.83
Total	**600**	**100**	**4.39**		**600**	**100**	**6.55**

Source: Ph.D. thesis P. Dhavamani, Madurai Kamaraj University, Madurai.

The SHGs in Orissa

In Orissa, Mission Shakti Campaign was started for empowerment and employment of women in the rural sector in 2001 to include 2 lakh groups by the end of 2008. But by 2005-06 it already covered 1.90 lakh and certain to reach the target as intended. Even though the number of groups declined from 2001-02 onwards by the year 2005-06 the saving deposits from the groups Rs. 68.44 lakh and loan amount disbursed to the tune of Rs. 256.62 lakh.

Number of groups along with savings deposits and loan advanced up to the 2001-06 is presented in Table 5.6.

Table 5.6

Growth of SHGs in Orissa: 2001-06

Year	*No. of groups*	*No. of members lakh*	*Cumulative*	
			Advances Rs. lakh	*Deposits Rs. lakh*
2001-02	41,475	5.57	15.34	13.54
2002-03	42,782	5.42	39.12	22.02
2003-04	35,737	4.39	113.20	35.48
2004-05	35,418	4.50	175.39	31.16
2005-06	35,373	4.15	256.62	68.44

Source: MSVN, Orissa.

The low status of women in large segment of Indian Society cannot be raised without opening up independent employment and income generating activities to cater there needs and aspirations. It is in this context, the need of the hour is to design gender sensitive development interventions which ensures the participation and involvement of women at every stage of development process from planning to evaluation.

✲ ✲ ✲

Chapter 6

WOMEN IN POLITICS

Women of India enjoyed exceptionally high status beginning from Rig Vedic age. During that period woman was not simply her husband's lifelong partner but also real partner in all his socio-economic activities including religious sacrifices. The Vedic word *Dampatti* denote jointly husband and wife that mean joint owners of the house. The girls like boy in those days underwent *Upanayana* of religious purification rites and given education like boys. But in later age the girls lost their status and Manu the great Hindu law giver discouraged this and the women relegated to an inferior position until the British arrived on the Indian scene that made efforts to provide equal rights to women.

Actually after India got Independence in 1947 the government is being seriously thinking about the empowerment of women in the country as it is firmly believed that unless the women are provided equal rights in the society in all the spheres they cannot participate in the socio-economic development of the economy. Empowerment of women involves three types of women's involvement in the society along with men.

Concept of Empowerment

Empowerment of women is a multi-dimensional and multi-faceted concept. It is the action and interaction of factors, socio-economic, psychological, attitudinal and political, etc. It is a process in which women gain greater share of control over resources, material, human and intellectual, and control over decision-making in the home, community and national affairs. Empower does not mean to give them power to dominate others or to use power to establish their superiority over others. In reality it is to empower herself and not to over power men.

1. ***Economic involvement:*** To induce the women into the economic activity they should be provided suitable education and also employment opportunities to participate in the economic development of the country. So far, these facilities are provided to women marginally and not in par with opportunities provided to the men.

2. ***Psychological:*** Once the women are economically independent, psychologically they feel self-reliant, attain higher self-esteem and gain confidence and try to actively participate in the social affairs.
3. ***Social participation:*** Once they attain economic independence, psychologically they feel in a better or in equal position with men, they can actively participate in different professions, and can actively involve themselves in the process of social change and decision-making organisations or in the political affairs of the country.

Three different important aspects of women's empowerment is presented in a schematic diagram in Fig. 6.1.

The Charter of the United Nations

The charter of the United Nations formulated three main goals for the organisation is:

- To prevent future wars by fostering peace and security.
- To promote social and economic progress.
- To protect the rights and freedom of every human being regardless of race, sex, language and religion.

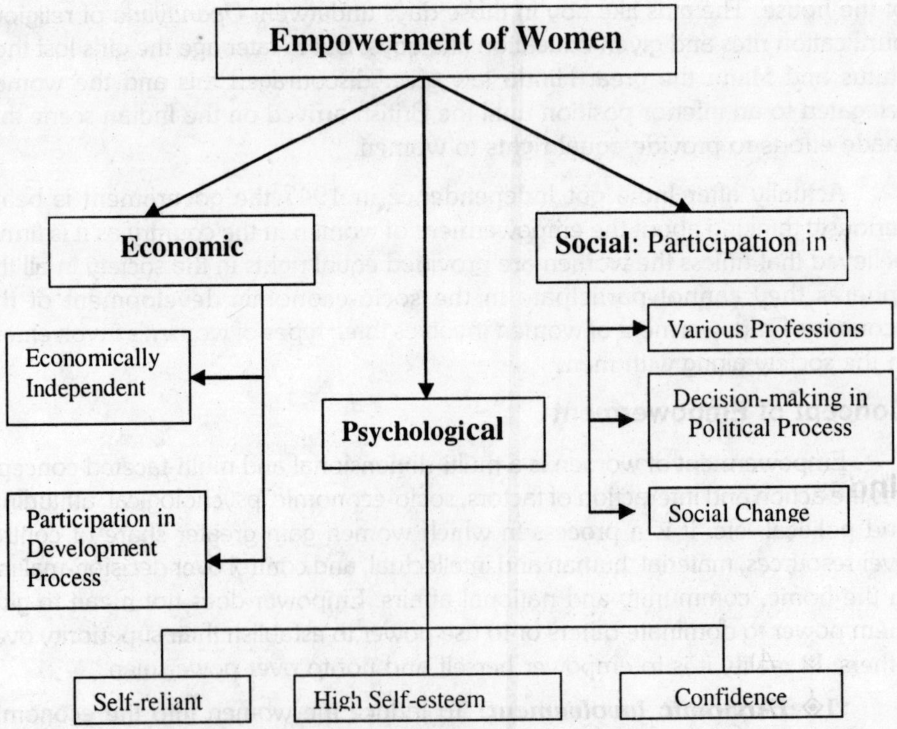

Fig.6.1: Different Aspect of Women's Empowerment

The charter reaffirms equal rights to men and women and explicitly asserts the three of the articles of the charter. The UN Sub-Commission on the status of women was elevated to the status of the Commission on the Status of Women in June 1946. The UN Social and Economic Council determined that the Commission on the Status of Women prepare recommendations and report to the Council.

1. On promoting women's rights in political, economic, civil, social fields,
2. On urgent problems requiring immediate attention in the field of women's rights.

At the global level continuous efforts have been made during the last half century to tackle the problems of human rights and to protect the rights of women.

- 1952: The convention on the Political Rights of Women.
- 1965: International Convention on the Elimination of All forms of Racial Discrimination.
- 1966: International Convention on Civil and Political Rights and Economic, Social and Cultural Rights.
- 1967: The Declaration on the Elimination of Discrimination against Women.
- 1975: UN declared the year as The International Year for Women and organised first world conference on women at Mxico. Later the world conferences held at Copenhagan (1981), Nairobi (1985), and Beijing (1995).
- The decade 1975-85 was declared as the UN Decade for Women to concentrate on the development and advancement of women.
- 1979: The Convention on the Elimination of Discrimination against Women.
- 1996: National Commission for Women and National Alliance for Women's Organisations come together and drafted "Women's Manifesto" demanding 30-35 per cent reservation for women in local, state and national level political institutions of the country.

Indian Constitution

The Constitution of India adopted in 1950 and later on amendments to it specifically mentions equality of sexes and equal rights in the political affairs of the country. The specific articles are:

- ***Article 14:*** Equality before law and equal protection of law.
- ***Article 15:*** Non-discrimination, *inter alia,* on the grounds of sex and the state has authority to make special provision for women.
- ***Article 16:*** Equality of opportunity in public employment.

- ***Article 39 (a):*** Equal rights for men and women to adequate means of livelihood.
- ***Article 39 (e) and (f):*** State directing its public policy towards the securing of health and strength of workers, men and women.
- ***Article 44:*** State endeavouring to establish a uniform civil code.
- ***Article 42***: Human condition of work and maternity relief for women.
- ***Article 51 A (e):*** Fundamental duty of every citizen to renounce practices derogatory to the dignity of women.
- ***Article 243 D (3):*** Not less than one-third of the total number of seats to be filled by direct election in every panchayat to be reserved for women.
- ***Article 243 D (4):*** Not less than one third of the total number of offices of chairpersons in the panchayat at each level to be served for women.
- ***Article 243 T (3):*** Not less than one-third of the total number of seats to be filled by direct election in every municipality to be reserved for women and such sets to allotted by rotation to different constituencies in a municipality.
- ***Article 243 T (4):*** Reservation of offices of chairperson in municipalities for the SC and SC and women in such manner as the legislature of a state may by law provide.

Joint Parliamentary Committee

The joint parliamentary party on the empowerment of women was constituted in 1997 to keep women's issues under constant review and monitor to watch progress in pursuance of plan of action evolved at international and national levels. The functions of the committee are:

1. To consider the reports of the National Commission on women and report on the measures that should be taken by the Central Government for improving the status/conditions of women in respect of the matters with in the purview of the Central Government.
2. To examine the measures taken by the Union Government to secure for women equality, status and dignity in all matters.
3. To examine the measures taken by the government for comprehensive education and adequate representation of women in legislative bodies, services and other fields.
4. To report on the working of the welfare programmes for women.
5. To report on the action taken by the Union Government and Administration of the Union Territories on the measures proposed by the committee.

Political Empowerment in India

Women's political equality in India emerged as political issue during the movement for independence of India from the British Rule in which for the first time the women of India came out of homes to actively participate in the struggle for independence. Never before the women of all walks of live participated in a movement along with the men and perhaps that was the first occasion for women empowerment in the country.

In this country Indian women for the first time in 1917 raised the issue of representation in politics. And for the first time the women demanded universal adult franchise and right to vote. In 1929 the women were given right to vote on restricted ground that they fulfil any of these three conditions of: (1) married women, (2) own property in their name, and (3) have education to a particular level. The Government of India Act 1935, passed by British Parliament allowed all women over the age of 21 to participate in general election and can vote for their candidate provided they have owners of property and got education to a certain level. In spite of the voting rights the women remained aloof from politics and it continued to be the male bastion. They continue to marginalise in decision-making bodies and remained invisible in political decision-making process.

It was the Committee on Status of Women in India in 1971 in their report demanded their grater representation of women in the political institutions; earlier the focus of women's movement was on improving socio-economic position. Among others the report recommended the following:

1. Establishment of Statutory Women's Panchayats at the village level,
2. Reservation of seats in Municipalities,
3. Constitution of permanent Committees in Municipalities to initiate and supervise programmes for women's welfare and development.
4. The political parties should adopt a definite policy regarding the percentage of women candidates in different political forums.

Political Affairs

The women of India, irrespective of their education and economic status in the society got the right to vote and participate in the country's political affaires. Providing simply the right to vote does not *ipso facto* make them powerful enough to participate in the political affairs of the country. They require certain other legal rights and social acceptance to participate in the governance of the country. Unless they actively participate in the politics of the country equally with men we are not certain that they got the power necessary to participate in the socio-economic affairs of the country. There is no doubt after independence few of women attained higher positions in the political system and some even moulded the political affaires of the country on a large-scale but these incidence are few and far between. It is not for India, it is also true for the developed Western countries where they boast of equal rights and opportunities for women. Proportion of women participant in our parliament and political parties of the country indicates that women are still far behind the men.

Women Members in Parliament

Women members in Lok Sabha from 1952 in the first Lok Sabha started will fourteen. Lok Sabha in 2004 ranged between 22 to 49 members, and latter number of highest women members are in the thirteen Lok Sabha for which election was held in 2004. In the present Lok Sabha the women members in Lok Sabha constitute 9 per cent of the total Lok Sabha members. In Rajya Sabha the position of women members are little better in the percentage terms. The number of members ranged from 12 (1952) to 29 (1980) and the highest percentage of membership 11.8 per cent in the latter year.

Women in Political Parties

There was only one dominant political party in India at the time of independence and in first general election held in 1952. Congress was the only national party to fight for the seats in the Lok Sabha, the lower house of parliament in India. Hence, all the women members of parliament were belong to Congress Party. In the first election after India become Republic in 1950, the Bharatiya Janata Party (then known as Jan Shangh) had only two male members in Lok Sabha get elected in 1952.

Number of women members in Lok Sabha and Rajya Sabha from 1952 to 2004 is presented in Table 6.1.

Table 6.1

Women Members in Lok Sabha and Rajya Sabha

Year	*Lok Sabha*		*Rajya Sabha*	
	No.	*Per cent*	*No.*	*Per cent*
1952	22	4.4	12	5.5
1962	34	6.7	17	7.2
1971	22	4.2	15	6.3
1980	28	5.1	29	11.9
1984	44	8.1	21	8.6
1991	39	7.4	24	9.8
1996	43	7.3	18	7.6
1999	49	9.0	—	—
2004	45	8.3	—	—
2009	59	10.8	21	8.23
Average	**34**		**19**	

Source: *Ministry of Information and Broadcasting, New Delhi.*

By the year 2004 there are now two national parties' equally important, the BJP emerged as second important party in India and also in Indian parliament. These two parties together contested 78 women members in Lok Sabha which constitute about 10 per cent of the total contestants. The other two national parties, namely, the CPM and Nationalist Congress Party together put up 101 candidates for the 2004 Lok Sabha of which 13 are women.

During the last half century ten regional parties emerged in the country and in 2004 election they together put up 1,013 candidates for Lok Sabha in which 72 are females which forms 7.11 per cent.

The women contestants in 2004 parliament election from different national and regional political parties and its percentage components are presented in Table 6.2.

Table 6.2

Women Contestants from Political Parties in 2004 Election

Party	*Candidates Fielded*	*Women Contestants*	*Per cent*
Congress Party	417	48	10.79
Bharatiya Janata Party	364	30	8.24
Communist Party (Marxist)	69	8	11.69
Nationalist Congress Party	32	5	15.53
Total	**882**	**91**	**10.32**
Bahujan Samaj Party	435	20	4.60
Samajvadi Party	237	24	10.11
Janata Dal (U)	73	3	4.11
Janata Dal (S)	43	4	9.30
People's Democratic Party	3	1	33.30
Triunamul Congress	33	6	18.18
Telugu Desam Party	33	4	12.12
AIDMK	33	2	6.060
DMK	16	3	18.75
Shiv Sena	56	3	5.36
Akali Dal	10	1	10.00
Rastriya Janata Dal	41	1	2.44
Total	**1013**	**72**	**7.11**

Most of the women politicians have no independent base in politics and have carrier of their own. Most enter politics as a sister, daughter and wife of some man who for some reason or others could not contest elections. It is difficult for women to establish a foothold without patronage from powerful men in the party. The glaring examples are, Mrs. Indira Gandhi could occupied the highest position of Prime Minister of India as the daughter of Jawaharlal Nehru or Mrs.

Sonia Gandhi the leader of century-old Congress Party if not the wife of Rajiv Gandhi. At the state level also the same theory applies with some exceptions.

Winning Women Candidates

The male and female contestants in different general elections to the Lok Sabha reveals that, in percentage term, the winning female candidates are always remained higher to that of winning candidates of males. In the year there was abnormal increase in the number contestante, a total 13,952 candidates contested of which female candidates were 599, all-time high as contesting election to Lok Sabha. At the same time the winning candidates in the election was also all-time low both for men and women.

It can be observed that in all the elections irrespective of number of candidates contested for the Lok Sabha elections the percentage-winning females exceeded the winning males. Another observation is that beginning from the year 1952 to the last election held in 2004 the percentage of winning candidates to the contesting candidates is gradually in the declining trend. In the 1952 election the percentage of winners both for men and women was 26.05 per cent and 51.61 per cent respectively. There were highest per cent of successful candidates, both male and female in 1957 election with 31.7 and 60 per cent respectively but the percentage gradually decreased to 10.00 and 14.00 per cent by the Lok Sabha election in 2004.

Contesting and percentage winning candidates of male and female in different general elections for Lok Sabha from the year 1952 to 2004 are shown in Table 6.3.

Not only the women representative's presence is negligible their representation in the council of ministers is also very poor. Between the years 1952 and 1975 India had only one minister in the rank of cabinet besides Mrs. Indira Gandhi. In 1980 there was no women minister in the rank of cabinet minister in Mrs. Gandhi's Council of ministers. There was only one minister in Rajiv Gandhi's government. In Mr. Atal Bihari Vajpayee council of ministers there were three cabinet ministers namely, Sushma Swaraj, Mamata Banerji, and Uma Bharti.

Table 6.3

Contesting and Winning Candidates in General Elections

Year	*Male Contestants*		*Female Contestants*	
	No.	*Winning Per cent*	*No.*	*Winning Per cent*
1952	1831	26.05	43	51.61
1957	1473	31.70	45	60.00
1962	1915	24.00	70	50.00
1967	2302	21.30	67	44.80

1971	2698	18.50	86	24.40
1977	2369	22.10	70	27.10
1980	4478	11.50	142.	19.70
1984	5406	9.20	164	25.60
1991	8374	5.90	325	12.00
1996	13353	3.80	599	6.70
1998	4476	11.20	274	15.70
1999	3976	12.30	278	17.30
2004	–	10.00	–	14.00

Source: Ministry of Information and Broadcasting, New Delhi.

A total of nine women ministers in Bajpai's Cabinet and it were the highest number of women ministers in post-independent India. Presently, in Dr. Manmohan Singh's Cabinet there are nine women members.

Representation of women in the state legislative assemblies is not satisfactory. The highest percentage of women in Madhya Pradesh assembly was 10.8 per cent in 1957. The average number of women representatives in the state legislatures ranged between 2 to 6 per cent of the total number of the members in the legislative assemblies. Manipur has lowest number of women representatives in the assembly of 0.3 per cent only. It seems there are no correlation beween literacy and number of women representatives in the state assembly. Kerala has the highest women literacy in India but their representation in the state assembly is 3.6 per cent on an average.

Percentage winning of male and female candidates for the Lok Sabha election from the year 1952 to 2004 is presented in Fig.6.2.

Women in Elected Bodies in Orissa

The representation of women in elected bodies is not satisfactory in Orissa. Out of 21 Lok Sabha MPs elected from Orissa only 2 are women in 2004 election. The Table 5.3 reveals that in 1951 there were only 3 MLAs out of 140, which increased to highest of 14 in 2000 but declined to 11 out of 147 in the state in 2004. Orissa was the first state to implement the 30 per cent reservation in local self-government bodies such as Panchayat Raj Institutions, Municipalities and Notified Area Councils.

Table 6.4

Women MLAs in Orissa

Year	*Total Strength of MLAs*	*Women MLAs*	*Per cent of Women MLAs*
1951	140	3	2.1
1961	140	5	3.8
1971	140	1	0.7

1981	147	5	3.4
1991	147	7	4.8
2000	147	14	9.52
2004	147	11	7.48

Source: Government of Orissa, Statistical Infomation on General Election to Orissa Legislative Assembly, 1990, 1995, 2004.

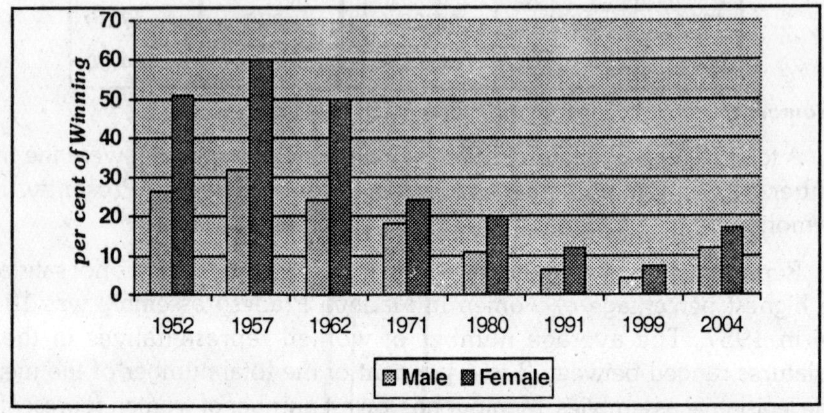

Fig. 6.2: Percentage Winning of Male and Female Contestants

Women in Dist. and Panchayat Level

The participation of women in rural development was first conceived by the planners from the beginning of the plan period in India since 1952. The community development programme started during the First Five Year Plan specifically given importance to the rural women. Subsequently continuous efforts were being made in involving women in the activities of rural development.

- In 1957 the General Council of Local Self-government resolved to co-opt two women members in the Panchayat Committee who are interested in working among women and children.
- The Balvanth Ray Meheta Study Team in the same year also recommended to include/coopt one or two women members in Gram Panchayat and Panchayat Samities.
- The Ashok Mehta Committee on Panchayat Raj accepted the recommendations of the earlier committees and suggested a mode of inclusion of women in the committee. The committee recommended including a women to contest for the membership but failed to get the necessary votes, the highest vote obtained among the failed candidates. If there are no women contestants coopt eligible women.
- The 64th Constitutional Amendment Bill in 1989 included 30 per cent reservation of women in the membership of Panchayat at the tree levels and also seat reservations for the scheduled castes and schedule tribes.

- The 73rd Amendment Act to Indian Constitution was passed in the year 1993 made provision for reservation of 30 per cent for women and provided substantial power to village women which was so far under the control of the government. This amendment facilitated the participation of women in large numbers to participate in the political spheres of at the district and below the district level in the Panchayat level.
- Five states gone ahead of constitutional provision of reservation of minimum of 30 per cent for women. The Government of Karnataka made highest of 46 per cent reservations for women in the Panchayat organisations.

Women in Panchayat Organisation of Orissa

In the Panchayat Organisation of Orissa in all the levels, district and Panchayat Samiti and in all the levels the representation of women ranged 33 to 36 per cent. Among women the SC and ST women also well represented in all the levels with 22.07 and 28.51 per cent respectively. Without the constitutional support the women might not come to this level at least in a backward state of Orissa.

Total number of members in the district and Panchayat level and share of women participants in all the levels presented in Table 6.5.

Table 6.5

Women Participants in Panchayat Raj Institutions of Orissa, 1997

Position	*Total Number*	*No. of Women*					
		SC	*ST*	*BC*	*RW*	*Total*	*Per cent*
Ward member	81077	6348	8060	6858	7329	28595	35.27
Sarpanch	5261	396	579	0	887	1862	35.39
Member Panchayat Samiti	5260	399	562	411	498	1870	35.55
Chairman Panchayat Samiti	314	29	44	0	41	114	36.31
Member Zilla Parishad	854	54	86	63	91	294	34.43
President Zilla Parishad	30	2	3	0	5	10	33.33
Total	**92796**	**7228**	**9334**	**7332**	**8851**	**32745**	
Per cent to Total		7.76	10.06	7.90	14.38	35.29	
Per cent to Women		22.07	28.51	22.39	27.03	100	

Note: BC=Backward Caste, RW=Reserved for Women.

Source: State Election Commission, Orissa, Bhubaneswar, 1997.

It is often seen that husbands and family members influence the women representatives in taking decisions. In most cases the women representatives are ignored and male family members invariably influence them. Another fact is that women members depend considerably on their men folk for decision-making.

The role of relatives of women representatives is sometimes taking active part in their official activities.

Myths about Women's Participation

A study made on the emerging leadership of rural women had identified the following myths about women's participation in the rural local governments at the Panchayat level:

- Women's passivity and disinterest in political institutions – where there are so many women to contest elections, etc.;
- Only the well-to-do, upper strata women will come through reservations;
- Their political connectivity – only privileged kins – women of powerful politicians will enter these institutions to keep the seats for them;
- Women who have entered the Panchayats are only proxy and namesake members. They do not participate in the Panchayats.

Due to reservation of seats for women in PRIs since 1992, there has been some improvement in the social status and empowerment of women. Major areas of improvement are as follows:

(i) Participation of women in Gram Sabha and Palli Sabha has increased.

(ii) Women PRI members are less corrupt as compared to their male counterparts.

(iii) For the first one or two years, the female PRI members act as per the direction of their male relatives (in most cases, the husband), but after that they act independently.

(iv) Female PRI members are more sincere than their male counterparts.

(v) Party-based political involvement is less in the case of women PRI members.

(vi) Women PRI members take more interest in the economic empowerment of women through formation of Self-help Groups (SHGs).

However, despite reservation of seats for women in PRIs many women do not come forward to contest elections owing to illiteracy and their inability to communicate with officials regarding grievances of their constituencies. Victimisation of elected women members, while claiming their rights is another important factor that creates hurdles in the process of political empowerment of women.

In majority of cases even if women have become chairpersons, but in reality all functional activities are being done by their husbands/male political mentors/ relations. This may be due to the lack of education, training, experience, social status and a large number of them are new entrants particularly from weaker sections of the society. It is necessary to build their capabilities to formulate and execute various programmes of economic development and social justice. Thus, a time-bound training programme is needed to make PRIs more effective and also for the overall political development of women.

73rd Amendment Act

In December 1992, Indian parliament passed a new amendment to the Indian Constitution to revive and revitalise the Panchayati Raj. This amendment gave a Constitutional mandate for democratically elected Panchayats at the village, district and intermediary levels in the whole country. The 73rd Constitutional Amendment Act of 1993 ushered in a new era in the political and social transformation of India. The amendment made provisions for delegation of substantial powers to villages, which hitherto were under the stringent control of both the Union and state governments. This legislation introduced reforms to the moribund Panchayati Raj institutions. Even though Panchayati Raj institutions have existed since independence, they were for all practical purposes non-functional because of lack of functional autonomy. Under 73rd Amendment, elections were made mandatory every five years. There were provisions of 33 per cent reservation of seats for the women, the scheduled castes and the scheduled tribes and other backward castes in proportion of their population. The 73rd Amendment was a step in the right direction by the government for empowerment of the people. The government felt that a democratic framework at the local level was indispensable for responsive administration. People at the grass roots level should be elected to manage their affairs through democratic decentralisation of power.

This amendment has facilitated the participation of women in large numbers who got the opportunity to contest from 600 district Panchayats, about 6,000 block Panchayats at the intermediary level and 2,50,000 Gram Panchayats. The 1993 Constitutional reforms were hailed by India's women's movement as a revolutionary action. Since then, almost a million seats have been put aside for women in Indian villages and district councils.

Thus, through this amendment based on the policy of affirmative action an attempt was made to empower women by ensuring their participation in decision-making in democratic institutions at the local level.

In the initial years, despite the stipulated 33 per cent reservation for women in local bodies, their representation was only symbolic, not widely known and definitely not acknowledged. Their male supporters who could be their fathers, husbands, brother-in-laws, brothers or others were managing the show. However, this scenario was changed in the last few years. It may be noted here that five states have exceeded the constitutionally recognised minimum, with Karnataka leading with over 46 per cent representation of women elected members in the panchayats.

Political participation of women is necessary not only for their development and improving their status, but also for their mass participation in national development. Political empowerment leads to their creative potential and make them economically independent. Threfore, there is a need to create political consciousness among women and motivate them to be active and participate in the democratic process.

❋❋❋

Chapter 7

VIOLENCE AGAINST WOMEN

Women's empowerment and agitations for the establishment of women's rights has been the main theme of the women's movement from the beginning of the 20th century. Violence was not the central theme of the women's movement until the 70s of the last century. The government and the social organisations came forward to give importance to the rights of women and issues of gender justice took importance with the women organisations, at the same time the incidence of violence in general and on women in particular become the concern of all.

Violence against women is an act of gender based violence that results in physical, sexual or psychological harm or suffering to women. The rights of women, her rights as an individual to defend any kind of violence are human rights, but discrimination based on gender, exploitation of her labour and breach of her right over her own body are inhuman and subhuman activities.

Violence on women can be classified into two groups: (1) violence within the family, and (2) violence within the society at large.

Violence within the family: All types of abusing the female folk within the family and house are coming under this category, such as:

- Beating and abusing the wife and engaging in all sorts of housework like a slave and mercilessly beating for every small mistake of her.
- Torturing the wife for not bringing sufficient dowry from her parents, forced her for suicide or beat her to death.
- Sexual abuse of the children and incest in the family at all stages of women's life.
- Female foeticide and infanticide and destruction of unwanted pregnancy.
- Alcoholism and marital rape.

- Impact of patriarchal values and domination and control within the family.

Violence within the Society:

All types of violence outside the house and in the workplace come under this type of violence: Violence and abuses against women can be classified into these categories:

1. Physical violence, including threats of violence, hitting with fists or weapons, with or without physical injury, is the most commonly understood form of abuse. All forms of physical violence are crimes under the *Criminal Code.*
2. Sexual violence is any form of non-consensual or forced sexual activity or touching, including rape. All forms of sexual violence are crimes under the *Criminal Code.* The term "sexual assault" encompasses a wide range of criminal acts ranging from unwanted sexual touching to sexual violence involving weapons, and is categorised according to three levels of severity. The term "sexual offence" refers to the three levels of sexual assault as well as other sexual offences which are designed primarily to protect children.
3. Psychological or emotional abuse includes insults, humiliation, put-downs and yelling, and extreme jealousy. These are not crimes under the *Criminal Code,* but are often effectively used to control and intimidate intimate partners. It also includes harming pets and damaging property, which are crimes under the *Criminal Code.*
4. Financial abuse, also referred to as economic abuse or material exploitation, includes restricting access to family resources, inheritance or employment opportunities, or to seize pay cheques. Unless theft, fraud or some form of coercion is used, financial abuse is not a crime under the *Criminal Code.*
5. Spousal abuse refers to physical or sexual violence or psychological or financial abuse within current or former marital or common-law relationships, including same-sex spousal relationships. The broader category of intimate partner abuse encompasses spousal violence and violence committed by current or former dating partners.
6. Spousal assault is measured according to the *Criminal Code* and includes physical or sexual assault and threats of violence.
7. Spousal homicide refers to the killing of a marital or common-law partner and includes first and second degree murder and manslaughter.
8. Criminal harassment/stalking is obsessive behaviour directed towards another person. It can involve persistent, malicious and unwanted surveillance, and invasion of privacy that is a constant threat to the victim's personal security. Criminal harassment is an offence under the *Criminal Code.*

9. Trafficking in persons is a crime under the *Criminal Code.* Trafficking is the use of deception, coercion or force to recruit, move or hold a person in order to use or exploit that person against their will for the sex trade or forced labour. The majority of transnational victims are trafficked into commercial sexual exploitation. These estimates exclude millions of persons who are trafficked within their own national borders (US State Department 2005).

Rape of Women:

In 1953 rape formed merely 0.41 per cent of 6.02 lakh total crimes in India, which increased to 1.03 per cent in 2006, of the total crimes of 18.78 lakh. Rape formed fifth position among the major violence against women in 1953 which increased to third position in 2006. In percentage terms there was 6.78 per cent increase in rape cases between the years of 1953 and 2006, which has the highest annual growth rate among the crimes in India. Abduction is in the third position among the crimes against women, with an average annual growth of 6.85 per cent in 52 years from 1953 to 2006. It formed 1.28 per cent of the total crimes in India in the year 2006. It is found that as many as 18 women are assulted in some form or other.

The important crimes and its annual growth rate between the years 1953 and 2006 are presented in Table 7.1.

Table 7.1

Rape and Other Important Crimes in India

Crime	*1953*	*2006*	*Average Annual Growth rate Per cent*
Rape	2,487	19,348	13.04
Abduction	5,261	23,991	6.85
Murder	9,802	32,481	4.44
Dacoit	5,579	4,747	-0.29
Robbery	8,407	18,456	2.31
Others	5,70,428	17,79,270	4.08
Total	**6,01,964**	**18,78,293**	**4.08**

Source: National Crime Records Bureau, 2007.

Dowry Deaths:

The dowry system is not specific in Hindu marriages. It was prevailed also in the Western world. In Homeric times, the usual Greek practice was to give a bride price, and dowries were also exchanged in the later classical time (5th century BC). Ancient Romans also practised dowry, though Tacitus notes that the Germanic tribes practised the reverse custom of the dowry. Dowry was widely practised in

Europe at all times. In Victorian England, it was seen as an early payment of her inheritance, such that only daughters who had not received their dowry were entitled to part of the estate when their parents died, and if the couple died without children, the dowry was returned to the bride's family.

Failure to provide a customary, or agreed-upon, dowry could call off a marriage. William Shakespeare made use of this in King Lear: one of Cordelia's wooers ceases to woo her on hearing that King Lear will give her no dowry. And in *Measure for Measure*, Claudio and Juliet's premarital sex was brought about by their families' wrangling over dowry after the betrothal and Angelo's motive for forswearing his betrothal with Mariana is the loss of her dowry at sea. Folklorists often interpret the fairy tale *Cinderella* as the competition between the stepmother and the stepdaughter for resources, which may include the need to provide a dowry. Gioacchino Rossini's opera *La Cenerentola* makes this economic basis explicit: Don Magnifico wishes to make his own daughters' dowry larger, to attract a grandeur match, which is impossible if he must provide a third dowry. One common penalty for the kidnapping and rape of unmarried women was that the abductor or rapist had to provide the woman's dowry, which was until the late 20th century the wreath money, or the breach of promise.

Providing dowries for poor women was regarded as a form of charity. The custom of Christmas stockings springs from a legend of St. Nicholas, in which he threw gold in the stockings of three poor sisters, thus providing for their dowries. St. Elizabeth of Portugal and St. Martin de Porres were particularly noted for providing such dowries, and the Arch confraternity of the Annunciation, a Roman charity dedicated to providing dowries, received the entire estate of Pope Urban VII. In some parts of Europe, *land dowries* were common. In Grafschaft Bentheim, for instance, it was not uncommon for people who had no sons to give a land dowry to their new son-in-law with the condition that the groom would take the surname of his bride. In some cases, nuns would be required to bring a dowry when joining a convent. In Europe and Western culture in general it is still common for the bride's family to pay for the majority of the wedding costs.

Provision for the dowry is described in the oldest records, such as the Code of Hammurabi as a pre-existing custom, prescribing only regulations for how it was to be handled and also included regulations for a bride price. If a woman died without sons, her husband had to refund the dowry but could deduct the value of the bride price; the dowry would normally have been the larger of the sums. It marks the first record of long-lasting customs, such as the wife being entitled to her dowry at her husband's death as part of her dowry, her dowry being inheritable only by her own children, not by her husband's children by other women, and a woman not being entitled to a (subsequent) inheritance if her father had provided her dowry in marriage.

The bestowing of dowries is an ancient Indian tradition most commonly observed in Northern India but seen across several regions of the country. It is social phenomenon that originated in the upper castes of India but eventually pervaded all socio-economic classes. "*Stridhan*" refers to a bride receiving jewellery or clothing from friends or family at the time of marriage. This should not be confused with "*Kanyadan*", which refers to the ritual of "giving away the bride", ceremony that is usually performed by the bride's father. In recent years, owing to strict anti-dowry laws collected in Article 498A of the Indian Penal Code, coupled with effective police action and increased social awareness, the practice of dowry has taken a very significant hit, though there are parts of the country where the custom endures.

A very well documented practice in ancient India, particularly among the princely classes was that of "*Swayamvara*", which may be translated as "choosing a husband by oneself". As part of this practice, the bride's father invited several suitors to a public ceremony, where the bride would survey them one-by-one and indicate her choice by putting a garland around his neck. In India, when a woman marries she then becomes a part of her husbands family. The family consists of her husband's parents, brothers (married or unmarried) and unmarried sisters. This is different from customs in more Westernised countries of the world where a man and woman typically begin to establish their own financial independence upon marriage. The additional financial strain an Indian woman places on her extended family obligates her family to pay a dowry. Dowry negotiations are all made verbally, and sometimes the demands for gifts will increase as the wedding day nears. Again, demands for dowry payments might continue indefinitely beyond the actual wedding. However, a distinction must be made between asking for a dowry and a request from the groom or his family for financial assistance. The failure to make this distinction has resulted in the abuse of anti-dowry laws. Recently, the Supreme Court of India upheld this distinction and spelled out clearly, in an instance where a farmer groom who was in dire financial straits requested his wife's family for help with buying fertiliser, that this was not a demand for dowry.

The husband and/or the in-laws determine the dowry, a gift given from the daughter's parents to the husband at the time of marriage. When the dowry is felt inadequate attempt is made to murder the new bride to make the husband available to remarry or to punish the bride and her family. In 1961, the Government of India passed the Dowry Prohibition Act, making the dowry demands in wedding arrangements illegal. In 1986, the Indian Parliament added "dowry deaths" as a new domestic violence crime. According to the new Section 304-B of the Indian Penal Code, where a bride, "within seven years of her marriage is killed and it is shown that soon before her death, she was subjected to cruelty or harassment by her husband, or any relative of her husband or in connection with any demand for dowry, such death shall be called 'dowry death' and such husband or relative shall be deemed to have caused her death."

There have been instances in which, if the father is unable to pay a handsome dowry, the bride puts herself at risk of abuse at the hands of her husband and in-laws. Although the bride's life may be in jeopardy, she often has no viable options of escape. Even a bride's own parents may express an unwillingness to take her back into their home. The cultural importance of 'family honour' has a lot to do with the parental reluctance to help. In India, it is considered disgraceful for a married daughter to return to her father's home after marriage. On the flip side, there is increasing concern in India over the rampant misuse of anti-dowry laws for harassment of the groom's family. In fact, in 2007, the Parliament noted that close to 11,300 false cases had been registered under the dowry Act during the year 2007.

The offenders can be sentenced for any period from a minimum of seven years in prison to a maximum of life. However, many cases of dowry-related domestic violence, suicides and murders have been reported everyday. The law could prevent these cruelties to women. A 1997 report claimed that at least 5,000 women die each year because of dowry deaths, and at least a dozen die each day in 'kitchen fires' reported as suicide. Prevention of bride burning is not an easy task which is now regarded as social evil. Stiff measures required to be taken on these lines:

- An increase in the standard of education for women, which will encourage economic and emotional independence;
- Proper implementation of existing laws along with new, stricter legislation to abolish dowry related crimes; and
- The establishment of voluntary associations to decrease the importance of dowries in general. Community-level programmes are essential, and must include doctors, who bear special responsibilities to help change the social milieu in which this phenomenon occurs.

The custom of giving and receiving dowry at time of marriage is an ageold practise, but in 20th century, especially in the second half, it becomes a social evil. This system often leads to (a) neglect of the girl's education, (b) the impoverishment of her parents, and (c) suicide of the girls in extreme cases.

The Dowry Prohibition Act, 1961 was further amended in 1984 and 1986 to broaden it to help both the parents and the bride herself. The Sec.498-A and 304-B are inserted in the *Indian Penal Code* and subsequent amendments in the Criminal Procedure Code (Sections 174(3) and 176) and Indian Evidence Act (Sections 113-A and 113-B) sought to strengthen the existing laws to curb the evils of dowry.

During the seventies of last century strong protest against dowry system gained momentum. There were strong people's movement asking for the rights of women. The trade unions and women's associations were the forerunners of the movement. Now the offence of dowry is treated as cognisable and non-bail-able and cruelty of others to the women driving her to suicide is punished. The dowry deaths are of two kinds, in the first case the bride due to torture commits suicide and in second case the in-laws and even the husband of the bride participate in killing the bride. But unfortunately the law could not curb the violence against women in their home. Torturing women at home rapidly increasing over the years, but number of dowry deaths are not declining; of course due to social consciousness and agitation of women's organisations the number of deaths almost remains constant in number. But in percentage terms the dowry deaths are gradually declining from 32.33 per cent to 17.21 per cent. It is also found that about 11.3 per cent of deaths of the brides are due to suicide.

The Economic Impact of Dowries

Generous dowries are a source of pride for a groom and his family because it, in essence, provides "bragging rights". Economically, dowries generate an increase in household income and wealth. Dowries can potentially relieve households of ongoing economic stress. By increasing the income and wealth of the marital household an elaborate dowry likely to minimises the economic and social stress experienced within a household. A dowry today is taken as a strategy for men to acquire higher standards of material wealth, status, and security. On the other hand, dowries have almost exclusively negative consequences on women's status, let alone their own survival among high status families, dowries are considered an essential part of "hypergamy", or, upward status mobility through marriage.

The Dowry Prohibition Act, 1961

This Act prohibits the request, payment or acceptance of a dowry, "as consideration for the marriage" where "dowry" is defined as a gift demanded or given as a precondition for a marriage. Gifts given without a precondition are not considered dowry, and are legal. Asking or giving of dowry can be punished by an imprisonment of up to six months, or a fine of up to Rs. 5,000. It replaced several pieces of anti-dowry legislation that had been enacted by various Indian states.

IPC Section 304-B: The dowry deaths law defines a "dowry death" as any of a wife in the first seven years of marriage without requiring evidence on a complaint that she had been put under unreasonable pressure to supply a dowry. It provides for prison sentences for over seven years for those causing dowry deaths. The usual practice is a three-six months of prison sentence on the basis of accusation.

IPC Section 498-A: Section 498-A was inserted into the penal code in 1983, it reads "Whoever, being the husband or the relative of the husband of a woman, subjects such woman to cruelty shall be punished with imprisonment for a term which may extend to three years and shall also be liable to fine". In practice, cruelty is taken to include the demanding of a dowry. This section is non-bailable, non-compoundable and cognisable on a report from a woman or close relative. This law makes it mandatory for the police to file charges against the husband, his parents and other relatives/friends named and put them in jail. There is no penalty or even a fine for filing a false case. Many individuals have claimed this is being abused by the wife or her close relatives.

In urban India, the majority of families have adequate knowledge regarding Section 498-A. Under this law, although both giving and taking of dowry is illegal, the dowry seeker generally faces greater punishment. The Malimath Committee in 2003, proposed making amendments to this section, although such amendments have been opposed by women's groups. The Centre for Social Research India has released a research report opposing amendments to Section 498-A. According to this report, in the studied cases there were no convictions based solely on Section 498-A although the report states that 6.5 per cent of the studied cases were falsified. They also state that many people believe the law has been abused by "educated and independent minded women". A police official asserted that in his district one-third of dowry murder cases were found totally false by the police. In 2005, the Indian Supreme Court declared Section 498-A to be 'Constitutional', while warning against its misuse, leading to "legal terrorism". They stated: "Dowry Law is a shield, not an assassin's weapon".

Several reports of the abuse have involved USA-based bridegrooms also. The United States Department states that a number of US citizen (men) who have come to India to marry Indian nationals have been arrested and charged with crimes related to dowry extraction. Many of the charges stem from the US citizen's inability to provide an immigrant visa for his prospective spouse to travel immediately to the United States. The courts sometimes order the US citizen to pay large sums of money to his spouse in exchange for the dismissal of charges. The courts normally confiscate the American's passport, and he must remain in India until the case has been settled.[1]

Sati System

Sati is another form of violence on women. In Sanskrit *Sati*, (the feminine of *sat* "true") was a Hindu funeral practice in which a recently-widowed woman would immolate herself on her husband's funeral pyre. The term is derived from the original name of the goddess *Sati* also known as Dakshayani, who immolated herself, unable to bear her father Daksha's humiliation of her (living) husband Shiva. The term may also be used to refer to the widow herself. The term *sati* is now sometimes interpreted as 'chaste woman'. With strict laws against *Sati*, the practice has become rare.

[1] In a well publicised case, Dr. Balamurali Ambati, who earned his MD at the age of 17, and his family were detained in India for over three years in a suit related to alleged dowry demands by the family for his brother's wife Archana, which delayed Dr. Ambati's entry to the ophthalmology programme for two years, leaving him to begin his residency in 1998. All charges against him were dismissed in October of 1996 and all his family members were acquitted in June 1999.

Few reliable records exist of the practice before the time of the Gupta Empire, approximately AD 400. Some instances of voluntary self-immolation by both women and men that may be regarded as at least partly historical accounts are included in the *Mahabharata* and other works. However, large portions of these works are relatively late interpolations into an original story, rendering difficult their use for reliable dating. Also, neither immolation nor desires for self-immolation are regarded as a custom in the *Mahabharata*. Use of the term '*sati*' to describe the custom of self-immolation never occurs in the *Mahabharata*, unlike other customs such as the *Rajasuya yagna*. Rather, the self-immolations are viewed as an expression of extreme grief at the loss of a beloved one.

The ritual has prehistoric roots, and many parallels from other cultures are known. Compare for example the ship burial of the Rus' described by Ibn Fadlan, where a female slave is burned with her master. Aristobulus of Cassandreia, a Greek historian who travelled to India with the expedition of Alexander of Macedon, recorded the practice of *sati* at the city of Taxila. A later instance of voluntary co-cremation appears in an account of an Indian soldier in the army of Eumenes of Cardia, whose two wives vied to die on his funeral pyre, in 316 BC. The Greeks believed that the practice had been instituted to discourage wives from poisoning their husbands.

Voluntary death at funerals has been described in Northern India before the Gupta Empire. The original practices were called *anumarana*, and were uncommon. Anumarana was not comparable to later understandings of *sati*, since the practices were not restricted to widows — rather, anyone, male or female, with personal loyalty to the deceased could commit suicide at a loved one's funeral. These included the deceased's relatives, servants, followers, or friends. Sometimes these deaths stemmed from vows of loyalty. Compare with later Japanese seppuku. Widow burning, the practice as understood today, was started to become more extensive after the end of the Gupta Empire, around AD 500. The rise of the practice has been variously ascribed to the decline of Buddhism in India, the rise of caste-based societies, and introduction by the Huna invaders who contributed to the fall of the Gupta Empire.

At about this time, instances of *sati* began to be marked by inscribed memorial stones. The earliest of these are found in Sagar, Madhya Pradesh, though the largest collections date from some centuries later, and are found in Rajasthan. These stones, called *devli*, or *sati-stones*, became shrines to the dead woman, who was treated as an object of reverence and worship. They are most common in Western India. By about the 10th century *sati*, as understood today, was known across much of the subcontinent. It continued to occur, usually at a low frequency and with regional variations, until the early 19th century.

Prevention of *Sati*

The Commission of *Sati* (Prevention) Act of 1987 Part I, Section 2(c) define *Sati* as: The burning or burying alive of –

(i) Any widow along with the body of her deceased husband or any other relative or with any article, object or thing associated with the husband or such relative; or

(ii) any woman along with the body of any of her relatives, irrespective of whether such burning or burying is claimed to be voluntary on the part of the widow or the women or otherwise. The Act of *sati* was supposed to take place voluntarily, and from the existing accounts, many of them were indeed voluntary. The act may have been expected of widows in some communities, and the extent to which social pressures or expectations constitute compulsion has been much debated in modern times. It is frequently stated that a widow could expect little of life after her husband's death, especially if she was childless. However, there were also instances where the wish of the widow to commit *sati* was not welcomed by others, and where efforts were made to prevent the death.

Traditionally, a person's funeral would have occurred within a day of the death, requiring decisions about *sati* to be made quickly. When the husband died elsewhere, the widow might still die by immolation at a later date. The *sati* ritual often emphasised the marriage between the widow and her deceased husband. For instance, rather than mourning clothes, the *sati* was often dressed in marriage robes or other finery. Her death may have been seen as a culmination of the marriage. In the preliminaries of the related act of Jauhar, both the husbands and wives have been known to dress in their marriage clothes and re-enact their wedding ritual, before going to their separate deaths.

Accounts describe numerous variants in the *sati* ritual. The majority of accounts describe the woman seated or lying down on the funeral pyre besides her dead husband. Many other accounts describe women walking or jumping into the flames after the fire had been lit, and some describe women seating themselves on the funeral pyre and then lighting it themselves. Some written instructions for the ritual exist. For instance, the *Yallajeeyam* provides detailed instructions about who may commit *sati*, cleansing for the *sati*, positioning, attire, and other ritual aspects.

Sati was supposed to be voluntary, but it is agreed that in many cases it may not have been voluntary in practice. Setting aside the issue of social pressures, many accounts exist of women being physically forced to their deaths. Pictorial and narrative accounts often describe the widow being seated on the unlit pyre, and then tied or otherwise restrained to keep her from fleeing after the fire was lit. Some accounts state that the woman was drugged. One account describes men using long poles to prevent a woman from fleeing the flames. Royal funerals sometimes have included the deaths of many wives and concubines. A number of examples of these occur in the history of Rajasthan. Maharani Raj Rajeshwari Devi of Nepal became regent in 1799 in the name of her son, after the abdication of her husband, who became a *sanyasi*. Her husband returned and took power again in 1804. In 1806 he was assassinated by his brother, and ten days later on 5 May 1806, his widow was forced to commit *sati*. There have been accounts of symbolic *sati* in some Hindu communities. A widow lies down next to her dead husband, and certain parts of both the marriage ceremony and the funeral ceremonies are enacted, but without her death.

Records exist of *sati* across most of the subcontinent. However, there seem to have been major differences historically, in different regions, and among different communities. There are no reliable figures for the numbers who died by *sati* across the country. A local indication of the numbers is given in the records kept by the Bengal Presidency of the British East India Company. The total figure of known occurrences for the period 1813 to 1828 is 8,135, another source gives a comparable number of 7,941 from 1815 to 1828 thus giving an average of about 507 to 567 documented incidents per year in that period. Raja Ram Mohan Roy estimated that there were ten times as many cases of *sati* in Bengal compared to the rest of the country. Lord Bentinck, in his 1829 report, states that 420 occurrences took place in one year in the 'Lower Provinces' of Bengal, Bihar and Orissa, and 44 in the 'Upper Provinces', the upper Gangetic plain. Given a population of over 50 million at the time for the Presidency, this suggests a maximum frequency of immolation among widows of well under about one per cent.

Jauhar:

The practice of jauhar, known from Rajasthan and Madhya Pradesh was the collective suicide of a community facing certain defeat in war. It consisted of the mass immolation of women, children, the elderly and the sick, at the same time that their fighting men died in battle.

Torture:

Torture of women in the household is in the second position after molestation forming 21.53 per cent of total crimes in 1991, while in the year 1996 it went to the first position with 30.44 per cent of total crimes in 1996. The growth of torture cases shown and an increase of 18.1 per cent, that is, annually on an average increased at the rate 36.25 per cent per annum.

Molestation:

The cases of molestation which was in the first position in 1991 with 20,611 cases was relegated to the second position after five years in the year 1996. In absolute terms the increase of these cases was marginal, while in percentage terms it slightly lowered in comparison to the figures of the initial years.

Sexual harassment:

The sexual harassment of all types of cases were in the fourth position in the year 1991, came to fifth position as a percentage to total crime. During the period, the growth rate of sexual harassment shown 18.37 per cent, at the rate of 3.67 per cent per annum.

Cases of violence against women in the country in specific categories are presented in Table 7.2.

Table 7.2

Violence against Women in India 1991-96

Year	*Rape*	*Kidnap*	*Dowry deaths*	*Torture*	*Mole-station*	*Sexual harassment*	*Total*
1991	9,793 13.22	12,300 16.60	5,157 6.96	15,949 21.53	20,611 27.82	10,283 13.87	74,093 100.00
1992	11,112	12,077	4,962	19,750	20,385	10,751	79,037
1993	11,242	11,837	5,817	22,064	20,985	12,009	83,954
1994	12,351	12,998	4,935	22,946	24,117	10,496	87,843
1995	12,922	13,543	5,151	28,835	26,134	10,943	97,528
1996	12,661 12.64	13,003 12.98	5,250 5.24	30,514 30.44	26,600 26.55	12,172 12.15	1,00,200 100.00

Source: Social Welfare, March 1998.

States' scenario

There are wide deviations of violence against women in the states. The four states which are in the forefront in violence are stated in Table 7.3. Dowry deaths and rape cases are highest in Uttar Pradesh where it formed 16.27 and 13.96 per cent respectively of total violence, the state which is comparatively a backward one. On the other hand in Delhi and Maharashtra where there is high component of educated people the ratio is very low. In torturing women Maharashtra, an industrial state with economically a forward one, shows highest percentage torture with 58.70 per cent. In kidnapping Delhi has highest percentage followed by molestation.

Table 7.3

Violence Against Women in the States 1996

State	*Rape*	*Kidnap*	*Dowry death*	*Torture*	*Mole-station*	*Total*
Maharashtra	1,408 9.62	940 6.42	472 3.23	8,589 58.70	3,224 22.03	14,633 100.00
Uttar Pradesh	1,741 13.96	2,562 20.56	2,028 16.27	3,649 29.28	2,484 19.93	12,464 100.00
Andhra Pradesh	771 11.28	581 8.50	432 6.32	2,597 30.01	2,452 35.89	6,833 100.00
Delhi	46 2.34	944 48.07	135 6.87	150 7.64	689 35.08	1,964 100.00

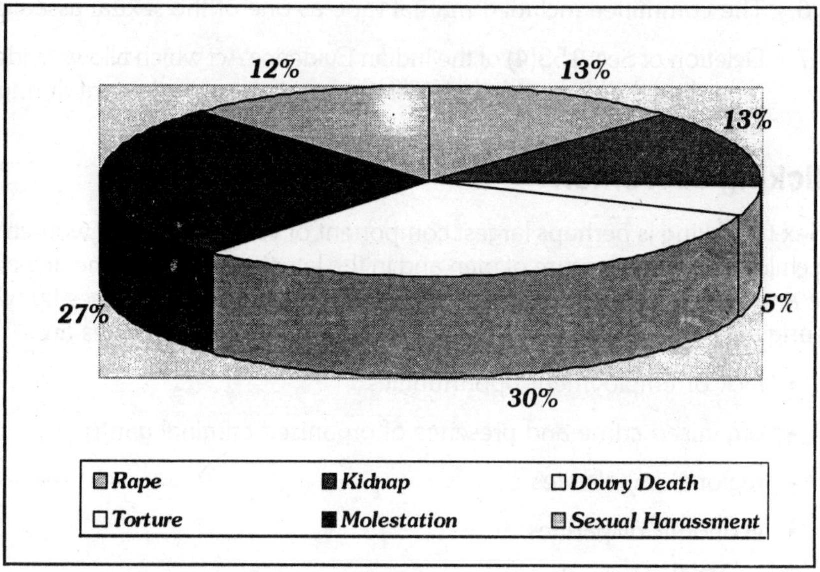

Fig. 7.1 Types of Violence against Women-1996

The National Commission for women

The National Commission for women felt that the entire law relating to sexual assault would have to be redrafted and very definition of rape and molestation in the *Indian Penal Code* is defective and archaic. A subcommittee appointed by the National Commission recommended the following to up date the present law to help the women.

1. The committee redefined and expanded definition of rape: Penetration into any orifice by the penis and penetration by an object or a part of body into the vagina or anus.

2. A lesser form of sexual assault known as molestation was also redefined which includes touching of any part of the female body for sexual purpose. It advised to replace Sec.354 of Indian Penal Code accordingly.

3. The committee also redefined exhibitionism and eve-teasing and included gestures, words and sounds with a sexual purpose.

4. Making a child perform various sexual acts was also included within the definition of sexual assaults.

5. The custodial rape was broadened and included other forms of aggravated sexual assaults: (a) A minor being sexually assaulted in a variety of ways, (b) Sexual assault on a pregnant women or on a female suffering from mental or physical disability, (c) Sexual assault by a person in opposition of trust, authority, social or economic domination, (d) Sexual assault which endangers the life of the victim.

6. The committee included marital rape as one of the sexual assaults.
7. Deletion of Sec. 155(4) of the Indian Evidence Act which allows evidence regarding the character and past history of the complainant during the trial.

Trafficking of Women

Sex trafficking is perhaps largest component of violence against women and young children for the pleasure of men and in the later age they become unwanted people and lead miserable life in the society. There are several causes by which the young girls compelled to opt for sex work. Some important ones are:

- lack of employment opportunities
- organised crime and presence of organised criminal gangs
- regional imbalances
- economic disparities
- social discrimination
- Uprooting of communities because of mega projects without proper Resettlement and Rehabilitation packages.
- Growing deprivation and marginalisation of the poor
- Insufficient penalties against traffickers
- According to the UN a major factor that has allowed the growth of sexual trafficking is "Governments and human rights organisations alike have simply judged the woman guilty of prostitution and minimised the trafficker's role".
- Driven by demand; demand is high for prostitutes and other forms of labour in host countries; therefore, there is a very profitable market available to those who wish to become handlers.

Trafficking in people has been facilitated by porous borders and advanced communication technologies; it has become increasingly transnational in scope and highly lucrative. Unlike drugs or arms, people can be "sold" many times. The opening up of Asian markets, porous borders, the end of the Soviet Union and the collapse of the former Yugoslavia have contributed to this globalisation of sex trade.

India is the second most populous country in the world, and an estimated 400 million are children between 0 and 18 years of age. Although acceleration in economic growth has made India among the 10 fastest growing developing countries, the country's per capita income remains low and 26 per cent of the population lives below the income poverty line. India is a source, destination, and transit country for men, women, and children trafficked for the purposes of forced labour and commercial sexual exploitation. India's trafficking in persons problem is estimated to be in millions. The Ministry of Home Affairs estimates that 90 per cent of India's sex trafficking is internal. Women and girls are trafficked internally for the purposes of commercial sexual exploitation and forced marriage. Children are subject to involuntary servitude as factory workers, domestic servants, beggars, and agricultural workers. Men, women, and children are held in debt bondage and face involuntary servitude working in brick kilns, rice mills, agriculture, and embroidery factories. India is also a destination for women and girls from Nepal and Bangladesh trafficked for the purpose of commercial sexual exploitation. Bangladeshi women reportedly are trafficked through India for sexual exploitation in Pakistan. Although Indians migrate willingly to the Gulf for work as domestic servants and low-skilled labourers, some later find themselves in situations of involuntary servitude, including extended working hours, non-payment of wages, restrictions on movement by withholding of passports or confinement to the workplace, and physical or sexual abuse.

The Government of India does not fully comply with the minimum standards for the elimination of trafficking however; it is making significant efforts to do so. India is placed on Tier 2 Watch List for a fourth consecutive year for its failure to show increasing efforts to tackle India's large and multidimensional problem. India's anti-trafficking laws, policies, and programmes focused largely on trafficking for sexual exploitation and the Indian Government did not recognise the country's huge population of bonded labourers, which NGOs estimate to range from 20 million to 65 million labourers, as a significant problem.

In the year 2006, the Central Government responded to the need for a Central Anti-trafficking Law enforcement effort by establishing a two-person federal "nodal cell", responsible for collecting and analysing data of state-level law enforcement efforts, identifying problem-areas and analysing the circumstances creating these areas, monitoring action taken by state governments, and organising meetings with state-level "nodal" anti-trafficking police officers. However, this nodal cell does not have the authority to investigate and initiate prosecutions of trafficking crimes across the country, as recommended by India's Human Rights Commission and Indian NGOs.

Three state governments established, with substantial US Government and UNODC assistance, the first state-level anti-trafficking police units in the country, which has led to an increase in rescues of sex trafficking victims and arrests of traffickers. The Central Government passed a law in October 2006, banning the employment of children in domestic work and the hospitality industry. In a July 2006 decision, the Supreme Court ruled that the Maharashtra Government could proceed with its plan to seal brothels under the Immoral Trafficking Prevention Act (ITPA).

The government prohibits some forms of trafficking for commercial sexual exploitation through the ITPA. Prescribed penalties under the ITPA-ranging from seven years to life imprisonment – are sufficiently stringent and commensurate with those for other grave crimes. This year, the government did not make significant progress in investigating, prosecuting, convicting, and sentencing those exploiting bonded labour. Despite the millions of bonded labourers in India, the government reported arresting only three offenders and confirmed rescuing only 26 adult victims this year. India, similarly did not report any criminal investigations or prosecutions of labour recruiters using deceptive practices and debt bondage to compel Indians into involuntary servitude abroad; the unchecked behaviour of these recruiters contributes to the forced labour of some Indians working abroad.

The government conducted at least 43 rescue operations in 2006 that released 275 victims of commercial sex trafficking from their exploiters; however, these operations were not accompanied with vigorous prosecution of traffickers. The Government of India provided significant in-kind contributions to a two-year US Government-funded UNODC project in Maharashtra, Goa, West Bengal, and Andhra Pradesh states, focused on raising the awareness of police and prosecutors on the problem of trafficking, and building the capacity of these police and prosecutors to investigate and prosecute persons involved with trafficking.

According to a study produced by the National Human Rights Commission a majority of traffickers surveyed claimed to rely on corrupt police officers for the protection of their trafficking activities. These officers reportedly continued to facilitate the movement of sex trafficking victims, protect brothels that exploit victims, and protect traffickers and brothel-keepers from arrest or other threats of enforcement.

Due to the intra-state nature of most of India's sex trafficking, the uneven response from state-level governments, and the lack of effective coordination among state police authorities, India should strongly consider expanding the Central MHA office to coordinate law enforcement efforts to investigate and arrest traffickers who cross state and national lines.

India may take following measures to prevent sex trafficking in the country:

- India should also significantly increase prosecutions of those arrested for trafficking, including employers who exploit forced labour, deceptive labour recruiters, and sex traffickers; and impose strict sentences on those convicted.
- Similarly, the government should significantly increase its efforts to investigate, prosecute, convict, and sentence public officials who participate in or facilitate severe forms of trafficking in persons.
- The Central Government reported no protection services offered to Indian victims trafficked abroad for involuntary servitude nor provides funding to repatriate these victims.
- The Government of India relied heavily on NGOs to assist sex trafficking victims, though it offered funding to these NGOs to build shelters under its Swadhar Scheme.

- The government should improve its protection efforts by enhancing the quality of rehabilitation services available in government run shelters.
- The Central Government did not effectively guard its long, porous borders with Bangladesh and Nepal through which trafficking victims easily enter the country. India also did not take adequate measures to prevent internal-trafficking for sexual exploitation or involuntary servitude despite the prevalence of such trafficking in major cities, and increasingly in smaller cities and suburbs.
- The lack of effective coordination between source and destination states, contributed to this problem, underscoring the necessity for a centralised law enforcement authority with intra-state jurisdiction.
- Services for bonded labour victims, and encouraging victims to assist in investigations of their traffickers.
- To address the issue of bride trafficking, the government instituted public awareness programmes to educate parents on the laws against sex-selective abortions and infanticide, and the negative effect that gender imbalance is causing in parts of India. While the Ministry of Overseas Indian Affairs instituted a system requiring women under the age of 35 going to the Gulf as domestic workers to obtain authorisation to leave India, the government failed to provide those travelling overseas with information on common trafficking perils or resources for assistance in destination countries.

According to the report of National Human Rights Commission (NHRC) a majority of traffickers surveyed claimed to rely on corrupt police officers for the protection of their trafficking activities. These officers reportedly continued to facilitate the movement of sex trafficking victims, protect brothels that exploit victims, and protect traffickers and brothel-keepers from arrest or other threats of enforcement. The government conducted at least 43 rescue operations in 2006 that released 275 victims of commercial sex trafficking from their exploiters; however, these operations were not accompanied with vigorous prosecution of traffickers. The Government of India provided significant in-kind contributions to a two-year US Government-funded UNODC project in Maharashtra, Goa, West Bengal, and Andhra Pradesh, focused on raising the awareness of police and prosecutors on the problem of trafficking, and building the capacity of these police and prosecutors to investigate and prosecute persons involved with trafficking.

The NHRC report observes these:

- Due to the intra-state nature of most of India's sex trafficking, the uneven response from state-level governments, and the lack of effective coordination among state police authorities,
- India should strongly consider expanding the Central Home Ministry's office to coordinate law enforcement efforts to investigate and arrest traffickers who cross state and national lines.

- Every year, an average of 22,480 women and 44,476 children are reported missing in India. Out of these, every year, an average of 5,452 women and 11,008 children are not traced. A recent report, *Action Research on Trafficking in Women and Children in India – 2002-2003* indicates that many of the missing persons are not really missing but are instead trafficked.
- A steady increase in the number of women reported missing. The rapid increase in the number of children reported missing that NHRC found really alarming. In Union territories like Pondicherry, there has been an increase of 400 per cent, while in states like Arunachal Pradesh, Nagaland and Tamil Nadu, the increase ranged from 100-211 per cent. In the metros, too, the figures are rising.
- In view of the possible linkages between missing persons and trafficking, the issue of trafficking needs to be given serious attention by law enforcement agencies, NGOs, the government and the community as a whole.
- Since information about missing persons is entered in the police station diary and not registered as an FIR, the follow-up is almost nil. There is a genuine requirement for integrating the police system with childcare services run by concerned NGOs. These agencies should take on the social responsibility of educating children and their parents about the steps that should be taken and the care that one should bestow upon children so that they do not go missing.
- The report notes that 40 per cent of the police officials were unaware of the growing trade in women and children! Traffickers usually target minors and Dalit women – the most oppressed group in the society. A study prepared on Bihar, says in the report that out of identified cases of women who had become victims of sex trade, 85 per cent were minors, and half were Dalits.
- Trafficking even though not reported from many places, occurs almost everywhere. The situation is worse in areas that are underdeveloped. Trafficking of women and children from the north-eastern states, and bordering countries – in both directions – is a serious issue that has not drawn public attention.

The NHRC report is the first of its kind in that it studies the long chain of trafficking from beginning to end. The Commission interviewed 4,006 persons in seven categories – victims of commercial sexual exploitation brothel-owners, survivours, traffickers, clients, trafficked children rescued from brothels and police officials – in 13 states and Union territories. Some of the revealing facts are shown in a tabular form in Table 7.4.

Table 7.4

Some Facts about Sex Trafficking

Particulars	Per cent
Started life in the brothel when they were less than 16 years	23
Age between 13 and 15	2
Promises for jobs	68
Promises for marriage	17
No savings	61
Girls below 18	21
Retrafficking	24
Health problems	32
Sexually transmitted disease	30
HIV positive	8
Clients preferred young girls	39
Married clients	45
Clients living with spouse	72

Human trafficking generates billions of dollars, and is globally the third largest source of profit from organised crime, after arms and drug trafficking. Several women and children trafficked are forced into the sex trade. The brothel-owners admitted that the highest demand was for virgins and confirmed that the highest profits came from children. The transactions in prostitution in India are worth Rs. 185 million a day, and Rs. 370 billion per year.

Protection of Women from Domestic Violence Act, 2005

The Protection of Women from Domestic Violence Act 2005 was passed by the Parliament in August 2005 and came into force from October 26, 2006.The primary objective of the Act is to provide protection to the wife or female live in partner from domestic violence at the hands of the husband or male live in partner or his relatives. The law also gives protection to those who are sisters, widow and mothers.

Domestic violence under the Act includes:

- Actual abuse
- Threat of abuse whether physical, verbal, sexual, emotional or economic.
- Harassment by way of unlawful dowry demands.

One of the most important features of the Act is the women's right to secure housing to reside in the matrimonial or shared household, whether or not she has any title or right in the household. The right is secured by a residence order which is passed by a court.

The Act also provides for appointment of protection officers and NGOs to provide assistance to the women with respect to medical examination, legal aid, safe shelter, etc.

The Act has been criticised on the ground that sometimes women herself plays a catalytic role in creating violence whether against the daughter-in-law, the mother-in-law or maid servants. Some surveys have concluded that 80 per cent of dowry complaints are false.

Four states namely Andhra Pradesh, Tamil Nadu, Uttar Pradesh and Orissa has ratified the Act on November 2007. Out of 8,000 criminal cases registered all over India under this Act Rajasthan had 3,440 cases, Kerala had 1,028 cases while Punjab had 172 cases. (http://en.wikipedia.org)

UNIFEM's (United Nations Development Fund for Women) Approach

UNIFEM works on several front towards ending violence against women and girls. This includes tackling its main root: gender inequality. Efforts are multiplied through advocacy campaigns and partnership with governments, civil society and the UN system. It works on legal framework to prevent violence at grassroot level. UNIFEM also involved in data collection on violence against women.

UNIFEM plays an active role in 'Unite to end violence against women' campaign, launched in the year 2008. Is another slogan 'say no to violence against women', 5 million signatures were presented to the UN Secretary-General. On behalf of UN system, UNIFEM manages the UN Truast Fund to end violence against women. (UNIFEM/Gender Issues/violence against women)

Violence in Orissa

Two of the very common violence against women in Orissa is (a) torturing for not getting sufficient dowry at the time of marriage leading to death of the bride, (2) rape and murder. The dowry torture and dowry death cases from 1991 through 1998 are shown in Table 7.5 in absolute terms both are increasing but in per cent terms to the total violence on women, torture on women is increasing while dowry deaths are in the declining trend.

Table 7.5
Violence and Dowry Deaths in Orissa 1991-98

Year	*Dowry torture*	*Per cent*	*Deaths*	*Per cent*
1991	214	58.87	161	75.23
1992	252	98.43	204	80.95
1993	376	61.84	232	61.70
1994	488	61.31	308	63.11
1995	565	61.55	353	62.48
1996	710	64.49	391	55.07
1997	727	65.79	378	51.99
1998	891	66.89	441	49.49

Source: Statistical Handbook of Orissa – 2005, Directorate of Economics and Statistics, Bhubaneswar.

Rape and Kidnapping

During the period from 1997 through 2003 the rape cases and cases of kidnapping, remained 772 and 490 respectively per annum on an average. During these seven years total of these two crimes increased from 1,187 to 1,239 an increase of 4.38 per cent; however, as percentage of total crimes in the state it remained almost constant with around 2 per cent. The figures are shown in Table 7.6.

Table 7.6

Year	*No. of rape*	*Kidnapping*	*Total*	*Per cent to total crimes*
1997	699	488	1,187	2.20
1998	825	511	1,336	2.13
1999	841	487	1,328	2.52
2000	778	441	1,219	2.25
2001	801	506	1,307	2.54
2002	707	512	1,219	2.39
2003	754	485	1,239	2.37
Mean	772	490	–	–

Source: Statistical Handbook of Orissa – 2005, Directorate of Economics and Statistics, Bhubaneswar.

The world health organisation reports that violence against women puts an undue burden on health care services and at higher cost, compared to women who have not suffered violence. Several studies have shown a link between poor treatment of women and international violence. These studies shows that one of the best predictors of inter- and intranational violence is the maltreatment of women in the society. Hence, a coordinated work among the government, NGOs and UN agency to combat violence against women through a variety of programme is the need of the hour.

✲✲✲

Bibliography

Ainsworth, M.K., Beegle, and Nyamete, A. (1995): The Impact of Female Schooling on Fertility and Contraceptive, LSMS Working Papers 110, Washington DC: World Bank.

Altekar, A.S. (1938): *The Position of Women in Hindu Civilisation*, Motilal Banarasidas, Delhi.

Approach Paper to the Tenth Five Year Plan (2001-2006): Planning Commission, Government of India, New Delhi, 2003.

Arputhamurty, Savitri, (1990): Women, Work and Discrimination, Asish Publishing House, New Delhi.

Basu, A. (1996): "Towards Ensuring Gender Equality", *Yojana*, Vol. 40, No. 1, January.

Basu, Aparna, and Bharati, Ray (1996): *Women Struggle: A History of the All India Women's Conference, 1927-1996*, Manohar, New Delhi.

Becker, Gray, S. (1964): Human Capital, New York, Colombia University Press.

Becker, Gray, S. (1998): Human Capital and Poverty, Religion and Liberty Archive, Chicago, University of Chicago Press.

Behrman, Jere, R. (1990): Human Resource Led Development, Review of Issues and Development, New Delhi, India: ARTEP/ILO.

Behrman, Jere, R., and Wolfe, B.L. (1987): "How Does Mother's Schooling Affect the Family's Health, Nutrition, Medical Care Usage and Household, Journal of Econometrics, 36.

Belenky, M., Chinchy, B., Goldberger, N., and Tarule J., (1986): *Women's Ways of Knowing*, Basic Books: New York.

Belle, D. (1990): "Poverty and Women's Mental Health", *American Psychologist*, Vol. 45, pp. 385-38.

Bhagawati, K. (2006): "Economic Empowerment of Women in India – An Analytical Study", *Journal of the Indian Economic Association*, 89th Conference Volume, Part-II, p. 1268.

Birdsall, N. (1993): "Social Development in Economic Development", World Bank Policy Research Working Papers, WPS 1123, Washington DC.

C.S.O., Government of India, *Statistical Abstract*.

Census of India – 1971, 1981, 1991, 2001, 2005-06.

Das, Sandhya Rani (2006), "Empowerment of Women: A Holistic Approach", In: *Mishra, Rabi, N., (Ed.), Women Education and Development, Discovery Publishing House, New Delhi.*

Das, Sandhya Rani (2008): Education and Economic Development – A Gender Perspective, Indian Economic Association, 90th Conference Volume, Part-I, pp.869-877.

Das, Sandhya Rani and Sharma, R.P. (2006): "Gender Disparity in Life Expectancy in Orissa", *Orissa Economic Journal*, Vol. XXXVIII, Nos. 1 and 2, January-June and July-December.

Das, Sandhya Rani, (1999): "Human Resources Development: An Analysis of Gender Dynamics in Orissa", *Vision*, Vol. XVIII, Nos. 3 and 4, Bhubaneswar, pp. 79-84.

Das, Sandhya Rani. and Sarma, R.P. (2008): "Quality of Life in Orissa – A Critical Gender Analysis", in Thakur A. K and Dalip kumar (cd) Gender Empowerment and Development Deep and Deep Publications Private Limited, New Delhi, Ps.

Das, Sandhya Rani and Sarma R. P (2009): Employment of women: A Gandhi an Model in Thakur A. K and Sinha Mithilesh Kumar Economics of Mahatma Gandhi: challenges and Development Deep and Deep Publications, New Delhi.

Datta, R., and Sundharan, K. (2002): *Indian Economy*, S. Chand Publication, New Delhi.

Desai, Neera, (1957): *Women in Modern India*, Vora & Co., Mumbai.

Desai, Neera, and Maithreyi, Krishnaraj, (1987): *Women and Society in India*, Ajanta Publications (India), Delhi.

Dev, M. (2006): "Gender Equality: An Analysis of Status of Women in India", *Journal of the Indian Economic Association,* 89th Conference Volume, Part-II, pp. 1042-1055.

Dubois, Jean, Antoine, and Beauchamp, Henry, King, (1897): *Hindu Manners, Customs and Ceremonies*, Clarendon Press, London.

Fogel, Catherine, Ingram, Woods, and Nancy Fugate (1995): *Women's Health Care*, Sage Publications, New Delhi.

Gaonkar, B. (1998): "Human Development via Empowerment of Women", *Journal of the Indian Economic Association,* 81st Conference Volume, pp. 248.

Ghotaskar, Sujata (1992): *Struggles of Women at Work*, Vikas Publishing House, New Delhi.

Goode, W. (1971): "Force and Violence in the Family", *Journal of Marriage and the Family*, Vol. 52, pp. 624-36.

Government of India (Planning Commission), *National Human Development Report*, 2001, 2002, 2005.

Government of Orissa, Economic Survey –1991, 2003-04, 2005-06.

Govt. of India: Economic Survey (2000-01, 2001-02, 2002-03, 2003-04, 2004-05, 2005-06, 2006-07 and 2007-08).

Guha, B. (2006): "Gender Related Development and Disparity", *Journal of the Indian Economic Association,* 89th Conference Volume, Part-II, pp. 886-900.

Gupta, Jaipal, Singh, (1996): "Literacy Accelerates the Pace of Development" Creations, National Literacy Mission.

Harbison, F., and Charles, Myers, A. (1968): Education, Manpower and Economic Growth, Oxford and IBH Publishing Co., New Delhi.

Hariharan, G. (1998): "Human Development and Gender Inequalities in Education", *Journal of the Indian Economic Association,* 81st Conference Volume, pp. 228-229.

http://www.educationforallinindia.clom

http://www.expressindia.com

http://www.ilo.org

http://www.indiabudget.nic.in

http://www.microcreditsummit.org

http://www.undp.org.in.

http://www.unescobkk.org.

http://www.wikipedia.org.

Human Resources Development Report, Orissa 2004 – NKCDS and Government of Orissa, Bhubaneswar.

ICDS, Bhubaneswar, A Report on Women and Work in Orissa (1995).

Jyotsana, Kamat (2006): *Status of Women in Medieval Karnataka*, Popular Prakashan.

Kalam Abdul, A.P.J. (2005): For Dignity of Human Life, Yojana, September.

Kate, Young (1998): Gender and Development – A Relational Approach, Oxford University Press.

Kaur, Manmohan (1985): *Women in India's Freedom Struggle*, Sterling Publishers Pvt. Ltd., New Delhi.

Kingdon, Geeta, Gandhi, (1997): Education of Women and Socio-economic Development *Baha'i Studies Review,* Vol. 7.

Kohli, A. (2006): "Gender Composition and Development: An Inter-country/Inter-state Analysis", *Journal of the Indian Economic Association,* 89th Conference Volume, Part-II, pp. 927-940.

Lal, O.P. (1992): "Watch Out, Food is Polluted", *Hindustan Times*, New Delhi.

Loung, T.V. (1987): "Women, Water and Sanitation", *Swasth Hind*, Vol. XXXI, No. 6, New Delhi, pp. 142-145.

Majumdar, R.C. and Pusalker, A. D. (Eds.) (1951): *The History and Culture of the Indian People*, Volume I, The Vedic Age. Bombay: Bharatiya Vidya Bhavan, p. 394.

Mathews, S.A. (1977): "Geography of Women's Health", Vol. 26, No. 3, Oxford, pp. 239-45.

McGranahan, G. (1991): *Environmental Problems and the Urban Households in Third World Countries*, Stockholm Environment Institute: Stockholm.

Mishra, R. C. (2006): Towards Gender Equality. Authorspress, ISBH 81-7273-306-2.

Mishra, Rabi N. (Ed.) (2006): Women Education and Development, Discovery Publishing House, New Delhi.

Mishra, Rekha (1967): Women in Mughal India, Munshilal Manoharlal, New Delhi.

National Accounts Statistics (2001): Central Statistical Organisation, Government of India.

Niraj, Kumar, (2005): Primary Education in India – Initiatives and Prospects, Kurukshetra, July.

Office of the Special Adviser on Gender Issues and the Advancement of Women, United Nations (August 2001).

Omvedt, G., *Violence Against Women: New Movements and New Theories*, New Delhi.

Padmanaban, K., and Sahayodoss, S. (1994): "Choice of Health Care Services", *IEA, 76th Annual Conference*, February, p. 66.

Perotti, R. (1993): "Political Equilibrium, Income Distribution and Growth", Review of Economic Studies, p. 60.

Peter, Adamson (1998): "Women's Health in Man's World", *Health Action*, February, Vol. XI, No. 2.

Phillips, D.R. (1992): *Health and Health Care in Third World.*

Primary Health Care: *Report of the International Conference on the Primary Health Care*, Health For All, Sl. 1, Alma Ata, USSR.

Psacharopoulos, G. (1984): "The Contribution of Education to Economic Growth: International Comparisons", Cambridge, Ballinger Publishing Co.

Psacharopoulos, G. (1994): "Returns to Investment in Education: A Global Update", World Development, 22(9).

R. Akila (2004): Reaching Global Goals in Primary Education — Some Gender Concerns for Tamil Nadu, *Economic and Political Weekly*, June.

R., Natarajan (2005): Internationalisation of Education in the New Millennium, University News, 43 (30), July 25-31.

Ram, Lily, Pitam, Telu (1981): *Environmental Health and Hygiene*, Vikas Publishing House: New Delhi.

Ranjan, S., and Azariah, J. (1989): "A Survey on the Quality of Drinking Water of Madras City and Public Health Information", *The Indian Geographical Journal*, Vol. 64, No. 1, Madras.

Rehman, Kante (1995): Gender Discrimination and Development Process, Labour and Development, Vol. No.1.

Salam, A., Md. and Shekher, N. (2006): "Gender Disparity in Literacy Rate in India: A Review", *Journal of the Indian Economic Association,* 89th Conference Volume, Part-II.

Sarma, R.P. (2003): Population and Economic Growth in "Dimensions of Population Growth", Edited by R.N.Misra, Anmol Publication Privte Limited, New Delhi.

Schultz, T.W. (1961): "Investment in Human Capital", American Economic Review, 51(1).

Seth, Meera (2001): *Women and Development: The Indian Experience*, Sage Publications India Pvt. Ltd., New Delhi.

Sharma, Radha, Krishna (1981): *Nationalism, Social Reform and Indian Women*, Janaki Prakashan, New Delhi.

Shramshakti (1988): *Report of the National Commission on Self-employed Women and Women in the Informal Sector*, New Delhi.

Singh, A.L., Fazal, S., Azam, F., and Rahman, A. (1996): "Income, Environment and Health – A Household-level Study of a City of India", *Habitat International*, Vol. 20, No. 1, London, pp. 77-91.

Singh, Avinas, K. (2005): University and Universal Elementary Education: Challenges and Opportunities, University News, 43, (47), November 21-27.

Singh, Panda, Rajender, Yadav, Susant, Kumar (2005): Education as a Fundamental Right: Need for Community Participation in Primary Education, University News, 43(25), June, 20-26.

Singhan, Gulabchand (1991): *Environmental Nutrition and Health Hazard in India*, Vohra Publishers and Distributors: Allahabad.

Tandon, R.K. (1998): *Status of Women in Contemporary World*, Commonwealth Publishers, New Delhi.

Tapan, Neeta (2000): *Need for Women Empowerment*, Rawat Publications: New Delhi.

Tarique, Md., and Sultan Z. (2006): "Status of Women in SAARC Countries: A Comparative Analysis", *Journal of the Indian Economic Association*, 89th Conference Volume, Part-II.

The Annual Reports of the Department of Education, Ministry of Human Resource Development, Government of India, New Delhi, 1985-86 – 2001-02.

The Annual Reports of the Ministry of Health and Family Welfare, Government of India, New Delhi, 1985-86 – 2001-02.

Tilak, J.B. (1989): "Education and Its Relation to Economic Growth, Poverty and Income Distribution: Past Evidence and Further Analysis", World Bank Working Papers 46.

UNDP (1996, 2001, 2004, 2005): *Human Development Report*, New York, Oxford University Press.

UNICEF (1991): Girl-Child in Orissa, Bhubaneswar.

Varkey, S., and Gupta, S. (2005): "How Gender (In)Sensitive are the Gender Related Indices?", *Bulletin of the WHO*, December.

Vianell, Mino, (1990): Gender Inequality: A Comparative Study of Discrimination and Participation, Sage Publications, New Delhi.

Women at a Glance. http:/www.un.org.

Women in Economic Activity: A Global Statistical Survey – 1950-2000, International Labour Organisation and the United Nations Research and Training Institute for the Advancement of Women, Santo Domingo.

Women in History. National Resource Centre for Women, New Delhi.

Women in India: A Statistical Profile (1997): Ministry of Human Resource Development, Department of Women and Child Development, Government of India, New Delhi.

Women Work and Child Care, UNICEF, Florence, Italy, 1992.

❋❋❋